Black Lions

Black Lions

A history of black players in English football

Rodney Hinds

SPORTS
BOOKS

Published in Great Britain by
SportsBooks Limited
PO Box 422
Cheltenham
GL50 2YN
Tel: 01242 256755
Fax: 01242 254694
email: info@sportsbooks.ltd.uk

Front cover designed by Kath Northam.

Front cover photograph by Getty Images.
Inside photographs, unless stated, from Empics.

A catalogue record for this book is available from
the British Library.

ISBN 1 899807 38 1
Printed and bound in England by Cromwell Press

Dedication

To Roy, Yvonne and Chantelle, my parents and daughter, whose love and inspiration has been a constant motivation. I will always be grateful.

Acknowledgements

University of Leicester; Norman Chester Centre of Football Research for their invaluable research, (Fact Sheet 4: Black Footballers in Britain), Kick It Out; Football Unites Racism Divides; the Scottish Football Museum, Phil Vasili; Paul Eubank; Professional Footballers' Association; Linda, heartfelt thanks, quite simply this project would not have got off the ground or been concluded without her input; Karyn whose inspiration (and office) was invaluable; Al for a quarter of a century of sporting inspiration; family, friends and associates who have constantly encouraged. This acknowledgement is not exclusive and I apologise to anyone who feels ignored and unappreciated, this is not my intention.

Sources

Vasili, (2000): Colouring Over The White Line, Mainstream Press.
Highfield Rangers, (1994): An Oral History, Leicester City Council
Woolnough, (1983) : Black Magic: England's Black Footballers, London
Longmore, A (1988): 'Black Revolution' in Football Today
Cashmore, E (1981): Black Sportsmen, Routledge
Hill, D (1989): Out of His Skin – The John Phenomenon, Faber
Leeds TUC and AFA (1987), Terror on the Terraces, unpublished monograph

Contents

Introduction

IN LESS THAN 25 years the black footballer has turned from freak show into a respected member of the football fraternity.

It was on 29 November 1978 that Viv Anderson strode out at Wembley to make the first appearance by a black player for the senior England side. Who could have imagined that by 28 September 2002 Arsenal Football Club would field nine non-white players for a Premiership fixture against Leeds United at Elland Road?

Both occasions confirm that the closed shop that was once English football has been opened up by players from the African-Caribbean community.

It has not been an easy journey. The sheer ability of black footballers has not always been the most important factor. They have needed as much mental and moral fibre to succeed as dribbling skills and backheels. as their colour and culture has been, and in some cases remains, a negative in some people's eyes.

While the black footballer has proved that the stereotypes attributed to him can now be kicked into touch, one important point has come shining through; as a collective they refused to be beaten on and off the field.

They have taken the abuse in their stride and given generations since the opportunity to partake in the national game with a more comfortable backdrop.

From the early pioneers, Andrew Watson, Arthur Wharton and Walter Tull, right through to Albert Johanneson, Clyde Best, Cyrille Regis, Luther Blissett, Garth Crooks, Ian Wright, Andrew Cole, Emile Heskey and Thierry Henry, there have been no shortages of battles to embrace and win.

Each one of the above has had to deal with the simple fact that the national game is a white working class activity which does not welcome uninvited guests with enthusiasm.

But the advent of television has done much to showcase the ability and character of non-white players. BBC TV's *Match of the Day*, which once illuminated fans' Saturday nights, quite literally set the ball rolling and Sky TV has taken coverage to another level.

Increasingly the displays of black players have been highlighted and what is clear in the new TV era is that non-white players have a lot to offer. The 2006 FIFA World Cup was almost a triumph for the French, a team with seven players with African-Caribbean backgrounds. *Les Bleus* may have fallen to the Italians at the final hurdle but TV highlighted more success for black players as did the creditable displays of Ghana and the Ivory Coast at the same tournament.

Put simply, while the TV revolution has made the sport accessible to all, it has done more than just provide football lovers with their passion.

The advent of football on TV has showcased the black footballer. Prior to the breakthrough of Clyde Best at West Ham United, black players had to endure a list of stereotypes. The litany of negatives was longer than a team sheet. It was said that they had an innate lack of discipline and consistency, chips on their shoulders, and could not perform unless the sun was out.

Those who followed Best, in his own way as influential as his namesake George, into the new TV era slowly but surely erased those negative views until today, around the world live, and TV audiences witness and indeed pay homage to black footballers.

Introduction

Whereas Best was aided by TV in his role as the leader of the enduring march of black players in the English game, the true trail blazers who played in England in the 1800s had no such audience in terms of numbers and admiration.

Andrew Watson, Arthur Wharton and Walter Tull, who led the black football revolution, had to cope with issues other than those just connected with football during their heyday. They encountered humanitarian issues too.

They had to deal with the cynicism and racism that society threw at them without the aid of TV coverage and anti-racist campaigns.

Watson, Wharton and Tull were eyed with suspicion and intrigue. What they did share with Best's day was the fact that this scrutiny was dominated by negativity.

But the fortitude of Watson, Wharton, Tull and Best, let alone their playing ability, has enabled those black footballers that came after them to kick a football, if not with total freedom, then certainly with fewer critics. Each black football generation that has followed has taken the baton with gusto to the point where black footballers are truly accepted in England and around the world.

But there still remains a shadow over the black footballer that refuses to go away. Until society in general accepts those that are different, football will not become a totally safe haven for black players.

There have been sadly too many negative statements by the likes of Ron Noades, Ron Atkinson and Luis Aragones over the last fifteen years for the black player to sleep comfortably.

When, respectively, a football club chairman, TV pundit and national team coach fail to give black players the respect they have earned, keeping a wary eye open has to be the order of the day for the black player.

In 1991, on the TV documentary *Great Britain United*, Noades, then chairman of Crystal Palace, suggested that black players were not able to do what white English players were able to do, especially in inclement weather. He should have been ashamed of himself.

After all, Palace were bolstered in the 1980s by the likes of Ian Wright, Mark Bright, John Salako and Andy Gray among others and have continued to give black players a window of opportunity.

Players like Wright and Gray served their apprenticeship as amateurs on bumpy pitches in South London, an arena in which black players still take terrible racial abuse in Saturday and Sunday Leagues.

I remember vividly watching an all-black side face an Essex-based team on the famous Hackney Marshes in East London many years ago. The match would have done justice to an amateur boxing bout as football was cast aside to be replaced by mistrust, violent aggression fuelled by colour, ignorance and misunderstanding.

Thankfully, I have not witnessed too many of those scenes over the years. Instead, I have seen players, officials, various football authorities and the media look to work together for the common good in terms of race relations. However, complacency remains the most dangerous opponent.

But it is when you see a black player's name on a replica shirt worn by a young white boy or a mature adult that you realise that one day football might be rid of the insidious crime of racism.

Black players, through their ability and charisma, have reached out to the aforementioned white working class community and proved time and again that, in the words of one of football's most popular chants, 'We Shall Not Be Moved.'

Chapter 1

Andrew Watson

WATCHING FOOTBALL NOWADAYS it would be easy to think that black players and their wonderful skills and athleticism have been around forever – and although this is not so, in one sense you would be right!

Arthur Wharton, who played for one of England's foremost clubs Preston North End, is often repres-ented as being the first great black soccer player. However, that distinction really belongs to Andrew Watson, born in 1857, in the then colony of British Guyana, and who won three international caps for Scotland five years before Wharton signed as a semi-professional for Preston in 1886.

Watson has long been forgotten despite a brilliant career that brought him silverware with Queen's Park, Scotland's pre-eminent team of the period, and his international honours.

The Scottish Football Museum, based at Hampden Park, uncovered the fascinating story behind Watson. His name links him to a Scottish parent, most probably on the paternal side with his mother being a native of Guyana; either African or East Indian.

Today the East Indians make up around 51% of the population of Guyana although in 1857 they were less common, being the first or second generation of indentured labourers brought from India. The next most populous group were labourers from Africa.

Little is known of Watson's early life in Guyana or

his first few years in Scotland, although research is ongoing. But his Scottish connection explains how he came to live in the country, where he joined his first club, Maxwell FC.

After that he moved on to Parkgrove in the Govan suburb of Glasgow. As a young up-and-coming player, Watson began to make a name for himself at Parkgrove.

The Scottish Football Association's Annual for 1878-79 listed him alongside some of the most notable players in Scottish football:

"Watson A., Parkgrove – Very fair back; tackles well, but a little rash when hard pressed!"

Watson was also listed in the 1878-79 Annual as match secretary of Parkgrove. He was living at 144 Buccleuch Street. Parkgrove's ground was listed as Trinidad Park, at Copeland Road in Govan, close to the present day site of Ibrox stadium, home of Rangers FC.

In the SFA's 1879-80 Annual Watson was still match secretary but had changed address and was now residing at 1 Rutland Crescent. His report now stated: "Watson A., Parkgrove – A powerful back, though deficient in tackling; works hard, and is an enthusiastic supporter of the game."

This snippet of information is very important. He was still a young player learning the game but was already making a name for himself. The reference to his enthusiasm for the game perhaps gives us an insight into his character.

Not only did he enjoy playing football, and not only was he ambitious as a player, he was also keen to promote the game and was very much involved as an administrator.

Andrew Watson

The match secretary was an important figure within the early football clubs, responsible for arranging fixtures with other teams.

Getting matches against the better clubs was desirable because it boosted crowd attendance, thus increasing revenue. Watson took on this role at the tender age of twenty-one. In 1879 the club had a firm membership base of eighty-five, fifteen more than Rangers FC. Perhaps it demonstrates Watson's own ability and enthusiasm that Parkgrove appear to have folded within a year of his departure for Queen's Park.

On 14 April 1880, Watson gained his first representative honour when he was selected for Glasgow against Sheffield. Glasgow won the match 1-0 at Bramall Lane. With Glasgow clubs largely dominating Scottish football then, as now, selection for the city's team was considered only slightly lower in status than selection for the international side.

Indeed, during this period the Scottish Football Association took full control over the Glasgow side. With this honour Watson's star was firmly in the ascendancy. Soon after the match against Sheffield, Queen's Park showed an interest in Watson.

The 'Spiders' in 1880 were still the leading club within Scottish football, capable of attracting virtually any Scottish player to their ranks. Watson's performances at full-back for Parkgrove had won him recognition and Queen's Park soon lured him to the south side of Glasgow.

The SFA Annual of 1880-81 was upbeat about the rising star of Scottish football:

"Watson A., Queen's Park, late of the Parkgrove.
– One of the very best backs we have; since joining the Queen's Park has made rapid strides to the front as a player; has great speed, and tackles

splendidly; powerful and sure kick; well worthy
of a place in any representative team."

A large number of black players have since adopted
Watson's template. Watson was also very adaptable
and could fit into a number of positions. Although
2-2-6 was the preferred formation of the late 1870s,
Scottish clubs like Rangers and Lugar Boswell were
already experimenting with 2-3-5.

Queen's Park, too, had adopted this classic formation
by 1880 and Watson, having just arrived at the club,
was played at half-back rather than his preferred full-
back role. The Glasgow Charity Cup tie against Vale of
Leven on 24 April 1880 featured Watson at right half
and in the final against Rangers on 8 May he was once
again in midfield; on both occasions Queen's Park
used a 2-3-5 system.

On 12 March 1881, Andrew Watson won his first cap
for Scotland against England at the Oval in London.
He was made captain and Scotland won the match 6-
1. Two days later he received his second cap against
Wales at the Racecourse Ground in Wrexham. The
Scots won 5-1.

Watson's third and final Scottish appearance came
against England on 11 March 1882. The match was
played at First Hampden Park and resulted in a 5-1
victory for the Scots. Watson as ever was solid and
consistent, the *Glasgow News* on 13 May reporting:

"Watson… was as is usual with him, very steady
and his speed aided Scotland to a great extent."

When you examine Watson's performances from
newspaper reports covering international matches,
Scottish Cup finals and Glasgow Charity Cup finals
his performances were consistently good.

It may appear surprising that Watson only took

part in three international matches – particularly as Scotland won them all, scoring sixteen goals and conceding just three. It is true to say, however, that there were so many talented players available within Scottish football at that time that it was difficult for players to gain a lot of caps.

On top of this Watson moved to London during 1882, presumably because of business commitments, and this would certainly have affected his chances of playing for Scotland.

At the time of winning his first cap, Watson was recorded in the 1881 census as residing at Afton Crescent on Paisley Road West with his wife Jessie, their son Rupert, and Jessie's sister Jane Maxwell. The census confirms his birthplace as Georgetown, Guyana, listing him as a British subject.

His occupation was recorded as a warehouseman. He was also honorary secretary of Queen's Park at this period and is listed as secretary of Queen's Park from November 1881 to May 1882.

In 1882, Watson was inadvertently involved in an SFA scandal. The minutes of an SFA meeting dated 29 February 1882 report an incident involving John Wallace of Beith Football Club, who was Vice-President of the SFA, and Walter Arnott of the Pollokshields Athletic Club.

Watson had been unavailable for a Glasgow match against Sheffield and the young Arnott was brought in to take his place. Arnott, however, was insulted by the remarks of the SFA's vice-president and wrote the following words of complaint to the Pollokshields' representative on the SFA Committee:

"You being our representative in the Committee of the Scottish Football Association I have to call your attention to the conduct of your Vice-President at Sheffield in his statements regarding myself which were uttered in the public smoking room of the hotel we were staying in before a number of gentlemen and also to myself personally that had Mr Watson of the Queen's Park been present and able to play at Sheffield he would have drugged me thereby rendering me unfit to play as one of your representatives at Sheffield?"

The remarks made by Wallace, although stupid, (they earned him the censorship of the SFA Council) give us an idea of Watson's status as a player. Arnott went on to become a legend with Scotland and, as a future Queen's Park player, he became Watson's teammate.

Prior to professionalism in Scotland, Watson, like any other amateur player, was not under contract to a particular club and although he was certainly a Queen's Park member for seven years he also guested for other clubs.

While remaining a Queen's Park member, Douglas Lamming reports (in a *Scottish Internationalists Who's Who*, 1872-1986) that Watson spent three years in London from 1882 to 1885, playing for London Swifts. He also assisted the famous Corinthians team during 1884-5. His presence in this select team is a sure sign that he was regarded as one of the best full-backs in the whole of Britain.

He played seven games for the Corinthians in their tour of Lancashire in December 1884 and one game against Notts County in January 1885. As selection for the Corinthians, founded by P A Jackson of the English FA to bring together the amateur elite and challenge Scotland, was by invitation only, it is a sure sign of Watson's importance.

Watson's debut for the Corinthians was an 8-1

thrashing of Blackburn Rovers, who were the English Cup holders!

His standing in the game at that time is also underlined by his presence in the Scottish Crusaders team which took on Aston Villa on 24 April, 1886. This little-known team was apparently an elite Scottish amateur team: a rough equivalent to the English Corinthians.

They did not seem to last long because Scotland remained an amateur country up until 1893 and in any case Queen's Park were already the elite team of Scotland, so there was little need for a Corinthians-style club.

In terms of football success, Watson won the Glasgow Charity Cup with Queen's Park in 1880, 1881, 1884, and 1885. Success in the Scottish Cup came in 1881, 1884 and 1886 (although the 1884 final never took place because Vale of Leven refused to play on the date stipulated by the SFA).

The current records note that he played 36 competitive games for the 'Spiders', as Queen's Park are still nicknamed, but as yet the total number of friendly matches is unknown.

The evidence of Watson's ethnic origins can be determined from a combination of sources. First, there is photographic evidence which clearly denotes Watson's ethnic appearance. The Scottish Football Museum has six separate team photographs featuring Watson. The 1881 census reports linking his birthplace with Guyana are also important.

There is another possible first for Watson: that of being the first black player in the FA Cup. He played for London Swifts in the Cup in 1882 and also in a first round tie on 31 October 1885 in a 5-1 win against Partick Thistle. (Although the FA Cup was an English competition, Scottish clubs were allowed in during the early years). Queen's Park scratched to South Shore in the second round.

In his book, Lamming comments that Watson was last known living in Bombay (now known as Mumbai) in 1902. No date of death is given. The museum is currently pursuing this line of research to determine what happened to Watson after he retired from football.

It seems clear that the facts gathered by the Scottish Football Museum establish that Watson was the first prominent black football player in Scotland and England, not Arthur Wharton as is usually thought.

On top of this, Watson was also the first known black football international and secretary in the world. Although there is still much research to be conducted, it appears evident that Watson's place in football history is undisputed.

Chapter 2

Arthur Wharton and Walter Tull

THE FIRST BLACK professional footballer in the Football League was Arthur Wharton. He entered the professional game in 1886, signing as a semi-professional for Preston North End before becoming a full professional with Rotherham three years later. In 1894 he signed for Sheffield United.

Signed initially as a goalkeeper, even though his pace meant he was also a more than capable winger, Wharton was in essence a good all-round sportsman. But even though he entertained hundreds with his sporting ability it is considered that he was never fully accepted because of his colour and he died a forgotten man.

Wharton was born in Jamestown, Accra, on the African Gold Coast (later to become Ghana) in 1865. Coming to England to study in 1882, he quickly made a name for himself in athletics. Still a student and running for Darlington College FC, Wharton won the Amateur Athletics Association 100 yards sprint at Stamford Bridge in 10 seconds, a performance which equalled the world best. He retained his title with 10.1 seconds at Stourbridge Cricket Ground in 1887.

After his triumphs at the AAA Championships he turned professional and won the unofficial championship by taking the September Handicap at Queens Ground, Sheffield, in 1888. A supreme all-round athlete, as well as athletics and football he was a fine cricketer and record breaking cyclist.

It was while playing for Darlington College as a goalkeeper in 1985-86 that Wharton was spotted by Preston North End. He joined them the following season during which they reached the semi-finals of the FA Cup. By 1889, he had turned professional with Rotherham Town, moving on to Sheffield United, Stalybridge Celtic and Ashton North End. He finished his footballing career in 1902 playing for Stockport County in Football League Division Two. His last match was against Newton Heath (later to become Manchester United) in February 1902.

Born into an upper-middle class family, his dec-ision to enter professional sport took him to a lower social level. He was rejected by the Gold Coast Colonial Administration for a civil service post because his sporting prowess was regarded as "inappropriate" for a colonial official. After he retired from football, he spent much of the rest of his working life as a colliery haulage hand in the South Yorkshire pits. He died in December 1930 and was buried in a third-class grave in Edlington, South Yorkshire.

During the 1894-5 season, Wharton played three games for Sheffield United's first team – in goal. This was not some quirk of the Blades' management to restrict one of the fastest men on earth to a small area at one or the other end of the pitch. He had played in goal for Darlington, Preston North End and Rotherham and, an unorthodox and entertaining performer, he had what was described as "a phenomenal punch" as a 'keeper.

He was enticed to Sheffield by Tom Bott, a United director and unofficial team manager. Bott had been Wharton's manager during his professional running days. What may have made Wharton's mind up was the additional offer of taking over the Sportsman Cottage pub in Button Lane. He liked a drink.

Unfortunately for Wharton, United had also signed a very promising nineteen-year-old – thirteen stone and growing – goalkeeper William 'Fatty' Foulkes. For the first time in his sporting life, Wharton could not dislodge his rival for the first team spot. He played only three games, against Leicester Fosse, Linfield of Belfast and Sunderland. In this last game, at Roker Park, Wharton made his debut in the First Division. The 'Cutlers', as the Blades were then known, lost 2-0. Wharton, the goalkeeper with the 'phenomenal punch', was at fault for one, his punching letting him down when he went to fist the ball away and missed it completely.

They say all goalkeepers are crazy, but during the 1890s a goalkeeper really had to be mad, bad or dangerous to know. Goalies could handle the ball anywhere in their half of the pitch and could be charged down with or without the ball. Trying to grab the ball in a crowded goalmouth, the goalie needed the protective and attacking skills of a Thai kickboxer. Wharton did not just punch the ball away, he had to get his retaliation in first.

Both Wharton and Foulkes were larger-than-life characters, similar men in many ways. Both were outsiders; Wharton because of the reaction to his colour and 'Fatty' because he was, well, fat! Both played in a very violent position and seemed to enjoy – indeed prosper on – the flow of adrenalin that surged after a punch-up with a few forwards in the goalmouth. Wharton was a womaniser. Did he and 'Fatty' ever socialise? We'll never know if they even spoke to each other, but goalkeepers at the same club often tend to be friends so the idea of the two being 'muckers' throws up some great scenarios.

Wharton was past his best when he joined United. He'd had a great career in sport, but the high points were the 1880s.

Wharton's greatest football moment was playing in the semi-final of the FA Cup in 1887 for Preston North End, then nicknamed 'The Invincibles', against West Bromwich Albion. Although hotly tipped to win the FA Cup, Preston lost 3-1.

Wharton also played professional cricket until at least his forties and in 1887 he set the record time for cycling between Preston and Blackburn.

There are few of Wharton's personal effects still around. His bible and a few photographs with his writing on are all that is left. He was lionised in the communities in which he lived, becoming a Northern working-class hero, despite his wealthy Ghanaian background. Like any other black person, he suffered racism, but he was not a passive victim. He was proud without being arrogant. And in 1897 he became a founder member of the Players' Union.

For 67 years his grave in Edlington Cemetery near Doncaster was unmarked. Football Unites, Racism Divides raised the money to fund the writing of Wharton's biography. Enough money was raised to place a gravestone on Wharton's plot – he is now visible once more.

Football Unites, Racism Divides is an anti-racism project supported by Sheffield United Football Club, which believes that football, as the world's most popular game, can help to bring together people from different backgrounds to play, watch and enjoy the game, and to break down barriers created by ignorance or prejudice. Their aim is to ensure that everyone who plays or watches football can do so in a safe environment, without the fear of racial abuse and harassment in either a verbal or a physical form.

Additionally FURD want to increase the participation of people from ethnic minorities in football, as either players, spectators or employees.

Walter Tull was born in Folkestone in 1888. By 1900, both his Barbadian father and his English mother were dead. Tull and his elder brother Edward were placed in a children's home in Bethnal Green.

Spotted while playing for the children's home team, he was invited to join Clapton, a top amateur team, in 1908. Helping them to victory in the FA Amateur Cup, the London Senior Cup and the London County Amateur Cup that same season, he was soon attracting the attention of other clubs. It was Tottenham Hotspur who moved in for him, playing him in their 'A' and reserve teams as a wing half. Still an amateur, Walter Tull was invited to tour Argentina and Uruguay with Spurs, signing as a professional on his return. After only seven first team games he was dropped. This may have been a consequence of the racial abuse he received playing at Bristol City. Rather than stand by Tull, the Spurs management consigned their young star to the reserves.

In 1911, Herbert Chapman, later to become a legend by managing Huddersfield Town and Arsenal to two championships each, signed him for Northampton Town, at that time in the Southern League, where he stayed until, like many of his contemporaries, he joined the army in September 1914. Serving in the famous 'Footballers' Battalion' – the 17th Battalion, Middlesex Regiment – he reached the rank of sergeant. Still able to play football when on leave, he guested for Fulham in 1915.

Recommended for a commission, Tull became an officer cadet in 1917. Commissioned as a second Lieutenant in the 23rd Battalion in the Middlesex Regiment, he was mentioned in dispatches early the following year. At a time of both an official and an unofficial bar on black officers taking charge of white men, his promotion was very surprising.

He signed for Glasgow Rangers but tragically did not live to make an appearance for the Ibrox side. He was killed in action during the German Spring Offensive of March 1918 while serving with the 23rd Battalion.

Chapter 3

Between the Wars

DURING THE PERIOD between 1919 and 1939, only a small number of black players came to the fore, playing for a variety of British clubs. Unfortunately, their efforts have either been largely unrecognised or forgotten, even by the clubs for which they played. Their experiences suggest that they, too, were the victims of racial prejudice and discrimination, both on and off the field.

Illustrative is the case of Jack Leslie, a London born Anglo-African player with Plymouth Argyle in the 1920s and 1930s. Leslie had made a strong impression as a goal-scorer, managing to score more than 130 in 400 matches for Plymouth between 1921 and 1935. He was once, erroneously, informed by his manager, Bob Jack, that he had been selected to play for England. However, he was never to make the national team. "He must have forgotten I was coloured," Leslie remarked ruefully later. Sixty years on from that humiliation, Leslie was still convinced that it was the fact that he was black that prevented him from making the England side. He was probably right.

In 1938, Northampton Town signed John Parris, who later went on to play for Wales, thus becoming the first black player to represent any of the home international sides. However, his achievements have not been widely celebrated. A player who could have equalled the prominence of Wharton and Parris, had not the war interrupted the early years of his career, is R H Brown, who signed as an apprentice for Stoke City in 1938. He did not make his league debut until the resumption of the League competition in 1946. He spent a year playing alongside Stanley Matthews, who was transferred to Blackpool in 1947.

Some Asian and African players arrived in Britain at this time and played in bandaged feet, as was their local custom. One such player was Abdul Salim, an Indian national, who was on the fringe of first team football at Celtic just prior to the Second World War. Tewfik 'Toothpick' Abdullah, one of a trio of Egyptians who played in the Football League between 1911-39, also played in bare feet for Sporting Club Cairo and the Egpytian Army. However, he managed to make the transition to boots, signing for Derby County in 1920. His two compatriots were H Hegazi, a centre-forward for Cambridge University, Dulwich Hamlet and Fulham, and M Mansour, who played in goal for Queens Park Rangers during 1938-39.

As football became more widely played within the European-colonised areas of Africa and Asia, so the potential supply of black footballing talent from those continents began to increase. In addition to this new development, the late 1940s saw the beginnings of an influx of immigrants arriving from the British colonies, most of whom had been persuaded to leave their country of origin in order to meet the growing labour shortage in Britain. This was to have an impact (albeit limited at that time) upon professional football in this country. As is, in many ways, the case with today's transfer market, the shortage of quality home players led to increasing competition and inevitably pushed transfer fees upwards beyond the scope of many clubs. This moved many club scouts to look abroad for less expensive. 'foreign' talent and thus increased the numbers of non-British born black players playing in England.

One of the most popular and successful African-Caribbean players playing in the Football League during this period was Jamaican-born Lloyd 'Lindy' Delapenha, who played for Middlesbrough between 1950-57. A great favourite at Ayresome Park, Delapenha managed to score ninety goals in two hundred and sixty appearances for the club, having previously played for Arsenal as an amateur and for Portsmouth during their 1948-49 League championship winning campaign, featuring in seven games.

Another black player who made his name during this period was Charlie Williams, who made one hundred and fifty-eight appearances for Doncaster Rovers between 1948-49 and 1957-58. Barnsley-born Williams was signed from local league side Upton Colliery in October 1948 and made his league debut the following season. He achieved even greater fame during the early 1970s as a television entertainer, starring in Granada Television's *The Comedians* and ATV's *The Golden Shot*.

In Scotland Giles Heron became the first African-Caribbean player to play first team football when he turned out for Celtic, scoring on his debut during the 1951-52 season. He was nicknamed the 'black flash' because of his speed. However, like many black professionals in Britain playing at this time, his achievements are almost entirely overlooked. Celtic's historical publications make no mention of Heron's time at the club. Heron was criticised in Glasgow for being unable to transfer his pugilistic tenacity to the football field. Heron had previously been both an athlete and a boxer but when it came to football he was described in the local press as "lacking resource when challenged".

Black Lions

Similar judgments made on the basis of racial stereotypes became commonplace and, as a consequence, black players playing in Britain became dogged with a purely negative image in the eyes of many top coaches and administrators over a number of decades. Heron went onto English non-League football with Kidderminster Harriers.

Perhaps the most famous black player in England during the 1960s was Albert Johanneson, a South African signed by Leeds United in 1961. A few years before this Leeds had signed another talented black South African, Gerry Francis, but it was Johanneson who made the bigger impact at a time when Leeds were establishing themselves as one of Europe's major footballing forces. According to *Yorkshire Evening Post* soccer correspondent Don Warters, Francis had only a modest association with the professional game in England.

Back in the mid-1950s he was determinedly saving what he could from his wages as a shoe repairer back home in Johannesburg until he had enough to pay for his own fare to England to try to break into English professional football.

He arrived in the 1956-57 season, when United, under the management of Raich Carter, had just regained First Division status after a nine year 'exile' in the Second Division.

Although Francis spent little more than four years at Elland Road, he made quite an impact in more ways than one. He was a popular figure with United fans. "I used to like playing best on the side where the old Lowfields Road Stand used to be," he recalled. "The fans there loved me and if I didn't get a lot of the ball the fans used to give some of my teammates a hard time for not passing it to me," he added.

30

In addition, his break-through helped pave the way for other South Africans, Johanneson being one and, more recently, United's skipper Lucas Radebe.

And Francis can also claim to have done his bit to help lay the foundations for the lifting of the players' maximum wage. Unrest among the game's professionals was growing and strike action was threatened in a bid to have it lifted.

He was signed as an amateur as United assessed his potential and performed well enough to be signed as a full professional in the summer of 1957 when he was paid a signing on fee of £10 and weekly wages of £12.

English clubs actually favoured white South Africans, feeling they would 'fit in' better in English football culture. At a time when the appearance of a black player at the top level in England was still very much a novelty, Johanneson was often subject to racial abuse, both by spectators and by opposing players. Such racism was often dismissed by club staff as nothing more than 'name calling'. Johanneson left the sun-soaked shores of South Africa to come to England which must have seemed like another planet. He had lived through the apartheid regime and on arriving in Leeds he was now ready to live the dream and a completely different way of life, alien to anything he had previously experienced.

He was born on the 12 March 1942 in Germiston, Johannesburg and was discovered playing football by a schoolteacher who had links with Leeds United. The club immediately offered Johanneson a three-month trial but Leeds United warned him that if his trial was unsuccessful, he would have to pay his own fare back to South Africa.

So while he was in England, his family and friends back home were busy organising fundraising events for his possible return. In April 1961, within a matter of weeks rather than months, he was signed from Germiston Colliers, becoming the late, great Leeds manager Don Revie's first signing.

He made his debut on the 8 April 1961 in a 2-2 draw against Swansea Town in front of 11,862 fans and made one of the goals, a pinpoint cross, which resulted in a headed goal for Jack Charlton, but the celebrations after the goal brought back horrific memories of his homeland. Johanneson remarked to a friend how he froze when the white Leeds players ran towards him in celebration. There was only one reason for a group of white men to be running towards a black man in South Africa.

He also had to get used to other traditions, which were a normal way of life in the football fraternity, such as joining his fellow Leeds players in the communal bath after a match. Johanneson for obvious reasons refused to join them until the players threw him in, a gesture which proclaimed he was now 'one of the lads'.

But before long he had to put up with racial taunts, not only from the terraces, but also from the opposition, many of whom did not bat an eyelid in calling him a 'black bastard' and other derogatory names in front of the Leeds fans, something that would not happen today.

It is rumoured that his 'minders' on the pitch were legendary names such as Billy Bremner and Jack Charlton, who stood for no nonsense in their protection of their black football wizard.

Another bone of contention for the South African was the weather; many times he had to be substituted until he became acclimatised to the conditions, but not once did the Leeds fans earmark him for abuse because of this.

In short, they adored Johanneson and every week they echoed the chant, "Albert, Albert, Albert, Albert". He obliged by scoring his first goal for the club against Rotherham United in the League Cup on 15 December 1961, some eight months after his debut, and scored sixty-seven goals in two hundred games, a remarkable tally for a winger.

Johanneson was a foundation stone of the 'Super Leeds' team playing with Bremner, Charlton and other iconic figures such as Paul Madeley, Paul Reaney, Peter Lorimer and Eddie Gray. For many years he was the scourge of opposing teams, who did not know how to handle this black South African with amazing football skills.

On 1 May 1965, he created history by becoming the first black player to appear in an FA Cup Final when Leeds lost to Liverpool 2-1, and he created many other records. In the 1962–63 season, in the former League Division Two, he broke the post-war record for the amount of goals scored by a winger in a season when he netted fourteen times. On 20 March 1965 against Everton he became the first Leeds United player to be shown scoring a goal on *Match of the Day* (which had become a national TV institution even though it was less than a year old).

He helped to create and sustain Leeds' image as a top European side from the very beginning. He was the first black player to play for an English club in a European competition since they began in the 1950s. An incredible achievement.

He secured his place in the club's history books on 26 October 1966 when he scored a hat trick in a 5-1 win over DWS Amsterdam in the Inter-Cities Fairs Cup. This was the first Leeds United hat-trick in Europe.

In *The Unforgiven*, the book by Rob Bagchi and

Paul Rogerson which recalls the story of Don Revie's Leeds team, it states how, after John Charles dep-arted from the club for the second time, Johanneson was to become an integral part of the revolution. It goes on to say that it is important to remember why he shone so brightly in Revie's first successful Leeds team of the early 1960s. It says, "For the next six years Albert was to provide the only element of glamour in a drab Leeds side". And that is why the Leeds fans again flocked to the fortress that was Elland Road in the 1960s.

Johanneson played for Leeds United until 1970 before joining York City for whom he played 26 matches, scoring three times and leaving in June 1972. Unfortunately towards the latter part of his career he suffered an alcohol-related illness.

In the late 1980s, he was 're-discovered' by the tabloid press living in poverty in Leeds, his years as a great local player forgotten or ignored. In September 1995, he was found dead in his flat. He was only 54. He died an early death, a great player allowed to decline in retirement.

On the 30 September 1995, 34,076 fans paid silent tribute to him before the home game against Sheffield Wednesday. Mike Casey, the chief sports writer for the *Yorkshire Evening Post*, paid a glowing tribute in his column 'Talking Sport' on Tuesday 3 October.

He wrote: "He was a trendsetter decades before modern idols like John Barnes, Paul Ince, Ian Wright and Les Ferdinand. Albert, having escaped the horrors of apartheid in his native country, bravely and uncomplainingly endured abuse from opponents as well as the terraces, as he added spice to England's domestic game. He never forgot his debt to the far sighted Don Revie who picked up a gold nugget in Johannesburg for the price of a plane ticket for his discovery. Years later, Albert a courteous, almost embarrassingly shy man told me: 'Mr Revie was like a father to me. I loved the man for what he did for me. I never really knew how it happened that I came to England. An agent dealt with everything. In London I was led off the plane by a stewardess to meet Maurice Lindley (United's assistant manager) and then it was onto a train to Yorkshire. I remember it was snowing and within days I was expected to play in the stuff I'd never seen before.'"

Casey added, "I can see Albert Johanneson shoulders hunched perhaps with modesty, ball seemingly tied to that lethal left foot, cutting past back-pedalling defenders as though they were figments of his imagination. Always good value for money, he would have been a star turn in this TV age."

Chapter 4

The Brazilian Connection

OTHER ENGLISH CLUBS, both professional and amateur, were also instrumental in bringing black players from Africa into the English game during the 1950s and the early 1960s. Watford signed a number of such players during this time, while Coventry City employed the Nigerian international Steve Mokone. Tranmere Rovers also had a Nigerian on their books, Elkaneh Onyeali, and Cambridge City had two African international players, John Mensah from Ghana and Francis Fayemi from Nigeria. Sadly, their impact on the English game was limited and did nothing to eliminate the racial myths which continued to dog black players over the following years. However, the increasing post-war immigration of black people to Britain was to have a profound effect on football particularly when during the 1970s and 1980s, the number of young black males born and raised in Britain increased substantially.

Those very same young black males were, however, to get their early football influence not from home-grown talent but from Brazil's legion of outstanding players. They may have been seen only on a TV screen but the impression they made on countless young men in England as well as the rest of the world should not be underestimated. The contribution of Brazil to the world of football is generally acknowledged. Their sense of style and supremely gifted footballers mean that they start every World Cup as favourites as the rest of the world watches and waits to see who their latest superstars are.

Over the course of five World Cup wins, the names of the great Brazilians roll off the tongue: Carlos Alberto, Cafu, Falcao, Garrincha, Gerson, Jairzinho, Pele, Rivaldo, Rivelino, Ronaldo, Roberto Carlos, Ronaldinho, Socrates, Tostao and Zico would all be contenders for a place in a World XI for most generations.

The success of these elegant, charismatic and talented players did much to encourage young black men in England to take up the game. Their success on the field of play, and the manner of their play, were the biggest draws for youngsters born in the 1960s and '70s.

Their first triumph, at the 1958 World Cup in Sweden, marked the debut on the world stage of the sixteen-year-old Pele, who would go on to be considered the greatest footballer of all time. Four years later, in Chile, they were to claim their second success, but it was in the 1970 tournament in Mexico that the Brazilians were truly to capture the imagination of so many young black men from the United Kingdom and beyond.

Pele and his gifted teammates beat Italy 4-1 in the final. The match was to be the great man's last World Cup victory but a third win at football's biggest showcase meant that Brazil were entitled to keep the coveted Jules Rimet Trophy.

Brazilian winger Jairzinho scored in all the six matches they played to rival Pele for star man status. With the 1970 World Cup the very first to be shown in colour, an impression was made on every youngster who had an inkling for the game. A whole generation of black Britons were now licking their lips in anticipation of a football career.

Black Lions

The mighty West Indies cricket team had not yet developed, so young black men in Britain saw Brazil as the very first 'black' team to taste global success. The legendary Muhammad Ali may well have been putting all his boxing rivals to the sword but he was an outstanding individual, so the collective success of the Brazilians was pivotal and should never be underestimated.

After the Mexico tournament, every playground was now full of Peles and Jairzinhos as youngsters attempted to re-enact some of the sublime skills of the South American masters.

Black football heroes such as John Barnes, Garth Crooks and Ian Wright have no hesitation in crediting the Brazilians for influencing their game.

Domestic football, too, was to get an airing on television. ITV had followed the BBC in recognizing the audience-attracting potential of the game and their Sunday show *The Big Match* was to be the showcase for Clyde Best during his days with West Ham United.

Best proved to be a powerful role model for many black youngsters. A powerful centre-forward born in Bermuda, he entered the first team at West Ham in 1969 and played alongside England World Cup heroes such as Bobby Moore and Geoff Hurst and briefly Martin Peters before he signed for Tottenham.

The first black Hammer, however, was John Charles, who broke the notion of a one-colour club at the Boleyn Ground. And by the early 1970s, West Ham United had a number of aspiring young black footballers on their books including Ade Coker and Clive Charles – but Best was the most promising. At a time of increasing television coverage of football, Best's exploits in the West Ham side were relayed to a wider public, which included an audience of aspiring, talented black footballers. A young black footballer in Leicester at the time remembered Best's influence:

"When I was younger there weren't any black players. I saw that football was dominated by white players and just run by white clubs, and stuff, and when I saw Clyde Best for the first time on TV as a black player it made me think, 'Black men can get into the Football League if they work hard enough at it'."

At the beginning Best was in splendid isolation at Upton Park, a ground in the heart of London's East End. It was not an area in which black people felt welcome, never mind one in which to put up their ability for scrutiny on a football field.

Best still remembers that when he arrived at Heathrow Airport in 1968 there was nobody to meet him. Then attempting to make his way to his new employers he travelled to West Ham tube station, rather than the more convenient Upton Park. History shows, though, that he got there in the end!

Without the contribution and fortitude of Best where would today's modern black superhero be? On 14 February 2004 Arsenal will be remembered for fielding a starting XI including their five man substitutes' bench made up entirely of foreigners. But until Ade Coker joined West Ham in the early 1970s, Best must have felt very alone. Coker made his name after scoring on a sensational debut as a 17-year-old in a 3-0 win at Crystal Palace in October 1971.

But it was Best, a fast, powerful forward, who almost single-handedly projected a positive image for black footballers. He made 186 appearances for United with a more than decent goals tally of 47. He paved the way for a whole generation to carve out careers in the professional game and his dignity against a backdrop of racist taunts is to be celebrated just as much as his goals.

The genial Best did not have the range of skills of his namesake George, but was generally loved by his teammates and managers. He recalled some of his most difficult times at Upton Park. "You've got to be strong. Ignore them. Carry yourself in the right manner. Show them the soccer ball does not care what colour you are. Give your answer by sticking one in the back of their net."

Best went on to play for Feyenoord, Ajax, Tampa Bay Rowdies, Toronto Blizzard and Portland Timbers. He was without doubt the finest player in the history of the Bermudan national team, gaining his first cap as a teenager.

In 1997 when Bermuda's football was at one of the lowest points in its history after seven team members were caught up in a drugs scandal, Best was appointed as national coach to breathe new life into the island's football. In a short period of time he had arranged Bermuda's first international on home soil for some five years. He was to knock his players into shape and restore some pride into Bermuda's football and footballers.

But the professionalism he had learned in England and during his nomadic football existence proved too much for those who ran the game in Bermuda. He was sacked in 1999 and despite the racial jibes he had suffered while paying for West Ham he suggested that he would have been treated better in England.

In 1998 Best was the star turn at a black footballers' dinner in Birmingham. Among those who descended on the Midlands, which shows just how important his contribution had been, were Luther Blissett, Garth

Crooks, Cyrille Regis and Mark Chamberlain who had all done their bit towards the advancement of black players but who recognised that on that special night they could pay homage to a man who had played no small part in their own careers.

Of that Best says: "I was introduced as a legend and players such as Regis and Blissett shook my hand and told me how I'd been an inspiration. When I see black kids playing in England and think that maybe I played a part in their emergence, that's my satisfaction."

The gala evening entitled 'A Tribute to the Pioneers of Black Football' held in Birmingham in 1998 was organised by Steve Stephenson, a pioneer of community development in the West Indian community. A keen sports lover, Stephenson, MBE, personal friend of such sporting greats as Sir Vivian Richards, Courtney Walsh and John Barnes, fondly remembers meeting Best, and the big man's cordial attitude.

He is in no doubt as to what today's modern players owe the former West Ham player. Stephenson says:

> "Clyde was a very nice person and never came over like the big footballer. I found him a most amicable person. He never behaved liked he was such a big legend.
>
> "I spent a bit of time with him at the hotel when he came over. He was very positive and he felt it was a great honour that we had actually chosen him to be the special guest and flown him over from Bermuda, paid his fare and everything. He was quite impressed.
>
> "Given the fact that the man is a legend in his lifetime he was very humble, a very warm person.
>
> "I think everybody that came to the event,

especially the players, were very pleased to be with him and a lot of the ordinary people too, really went out of their way to speak to him. My brother idolised him from the seventies. In terms of the experience it was phenomenal for a lot of people that they actually met this man. It was really good.

"I think the modern players at present like Rio Ferdinand and Ashley Cole and the rest of them owe Clyde Best an awful lot because if it wasn't for him and the other pioneers, many of the present players wouldn't be where they are. There was a myth one time that black players were afraid of the cold and that they had weak ankles and negative things like that. Modern footballers can't repay the likes of Clyde Best and Cyrille Regis."

Sadly for Clyde Best, he was never to reach the heights scaled by some of his white West Ham teammates. At a time when he was the only black player playing regular first team football in the English First Division, he was constantly subject to criticism and racial abuse. Brian Woolnough's book on black footballers, *Black Magic: England's Black Footballers*, published in 1983 is ostensibly, a celebration of black players in the British game but is, in fact, run through with racist assumptions. On Best, Woolnough commented: "He is perhaps the best example of why it has taken so long for managers, coaches and the public to accept the coloured (sic) stars. Best would be brilliant one game, bad the next, and the question marks against the black players' stamina, power and determination hung over them for years".

The racist treatment received by black players at this time from both spectators and players probably dissuaded many black parents from encouraging their sons to pursue a career in professional football (Longmore, 1988; Hill, 1989). Nonetheless, Best provided a platform which future black stars could build upon to become successful players.

Chapter 5

Viv Anderson's breakthrough

WHILE CLYDE BEST was flying the flag in London's East End, Cyril 'Ces' Podd was a trailblazer at Bradford City in Yorkshire. He was one of the first black footballers to establish himself over a long period in the Football League and went on to be one of the longest serving players in City's history.

Born in St Kitts, Podd moved to England to live with his parents when he was just nine years old. He progressed through local football and signed for City in August 1970.

A quick full-back, he made 565 appearances, scoring just four goals. But his job was essentially to defend, unlike today's modern full-backs who have licence to get into the opposing penalty area.

From Bradford, he joined Halifax and ended his career at Scarborough. One of his final task was to help Scarborough gain promotion to the Football League after more than a century in the lower leagues.

Podd's ability, despite the grief he was taking, would shine through most weeks. City's website suggests that mighty Manchester United were interested in capturing the defender's signature but the loyalty that had been shown to him by the club and certain sections of the fan base meant that he turned his back on United.

Podd was one of the first black players to prove

that longevity and consistency was not a problem for a black footballer. He took his fair share of abuse and Podd's mother has said that her son was often spat at while he was at work on the football field.

For keen young black football followers living in England during the 1960s, their local heroes were likely to be white English players. Internationally, of course, Pele, Eusebio, Garrincha and others would have been known to many black Britons especially following the 1966 World Cup finals, held in England. This local situation began to change during the late 1960s and early 1970s.

Gradually, as black participation in the British football world increased (as it also did in athletics and boxing), so too did the number of black role models, the focus of which would provide young black footballers in Britain with greater inspiration.

There were other black stars emerging at this time. Brendon Batson, the first black player at Arsenal, had had a brief flirtation with first team football in north London after being part of the youth team squad which won the FA Youth Cup in 1971; Ricky Heppolette starred for Preston North End and Leyton Orient and was probably the first ethnic Indian to break into first team professional football in England; and there was Cliff Marshall at Everton.

They had all entered a profession which was not in any way multi-cultural. Nor were they given much in the way of a warm welcome by some of their fellow professionals.

But the number of young blacks joining Football League clubs kept growing. At Nottingham Forest, Viv Anderson was a key member at right-back of Brian Clough's side which won domestic and European honours between seasons 1977-78 and 1979-80, and on

29 November 1978 he forever changed the course of black footballers in Britain.

On that decidedly cold night against Czechoslovakia, blunting the stereotype that black players could not handle intemperate conditions, Viv Anderson became the first black player to play for the full England side. It was more than half a century after Jack Leslie's 'false alarm'.

Having been rejected by Manchester United as a youngster – a club he would later join – Anderson established himself at Forest as Clough took the unfashionable East Midlands club from the middle of the old Second Division to the First Division and beyond to European glory.

After winning virtually all there was to win with Forest, Anderson joined Arsenal in 1984 before, in 1987, becoming Alex Ferguson's first signing at Manchester United, and at last fulfilling his boyhood dream.

But while his club career was noteworthy, it was the sight of Anderson with the Three Lions on his chest in November 1978 that will mark him down forever as a true pioneer.

He moved into coaching and football management after his playing days ended, first at Barnsley, then at Middlesbrough – one of the few black players to successfully make this transition.

Only now, when he manages a corporate sports company, does Anderson, awarded an MBE in 1999 for his services to football, appreciate the magnitude of his England debut. Always keen to downplay his achievements, like so many black players in the 1970s and '80s, Anderson was ill-prepared for the furore caused by a black man playing for the senior national side.

Viv Anderson's Breakthrough

He remembers:

"To me it was just a matter of playing and being on this big stage and getting telegrams of good luck from the Queen and Elton John and everything else. Who could prepare you for that!

"I wasn't there because I happened to be black. You don't prepare yourself for anything like that. I just wanted to play for my country and I was looking forward to playing the game. I didn't realise what an impact it would make at the time. Only now do you realise what an impact it did have. At the time I just wanted to do well.

"My mother didn't come but my father did. My father is the most laid-back person in the world. After the biggest game of my career he was like 'oh well' and that was it! On to the next thing, we were going home sort of thing. So, in our family it was dismissed very quickly with an attitude of on to the next one. Other people made a big thing of it."

As he was the first black player to represent the senior side, Anderson admits that he escaped some of the barbs that were to come the way of those that followed him. Players such as Luther Blissett, Cyrille Regis and John Barnes were to be threatened by the National Front and those that supported their doctrine. Considering that he was in isolation in the England starting eleven, Anderson got off lightly.

"Looking back at it there must have been some [racism] aimed at me but I was never the victim of that. You speak to Cyrille and some of the other guys around at the time, and they certainly suffered. I remember Cyrille getting a bullet through the post and stuff like that.

"The expectations of black players at the time were that they were flamboyant and couldn't play in the winter; they were only 'summer' players… Then I came along and with me it was just a case of run them down and kick them. That was completely different to the norm.

"As for being able to play in the cold, I never wore long sleeve shirts because I didn't like them. I always wore short sleeved shirts so I was completely different from everybody else. I don't know why it was that things weren't that bad for me. I was never really aware of anything.

"It was a strange night [his international debut] because one side of the pitch was rock hard and the other side was completely soft, so you had to wear rubber studs in the first half and ordinary studs in the second half. It was a really weird night. It was a strange debut to say the least.

"If you ask me now if I remember the game I have to say I am the world's worst person at remembering anything! All I remember is that I had a hand in the goal. I think I played it to Stevie Coppell and he scored. The actual game was a blur, even now. I can remember certain games. I can remember winning the championship with Forest at Coventry. Bits of it that's all, the European Cup, bits of it. The general thing just goes straight out of my head."

That Anderson carved out a thirty-cap career and won honours at home and abroad was nothing short of a fairytale. After his rejection by Manchester United during the formative years of his career he showed the resolve and tenacity that held him in good stead as he attempted to quell the threat of some of the game's quickest wingers. It would be fair to say that he put black players on the map in general and confirmed, at last, that they could put up with the physical side of the game and defend.

> "I would have been fifteen or sixteen when I was rejected by United. And then it was a big rejection but in hindsight if you think about it the club had all England internationals, Scottish internationals… they were all there, so they had the pick of the bunch. I was a skinny, little kid from Nottingham. Realistically, how was I ever going to get chosen in front of those quality players? Obviously I was disappointed because I went there for a year, going backwards and forwards and then, when I did go back to Nottingham, I got a 'proper' job because I thought that was the end of my football career. Every school holidays I was backwards and forwards on the train or my dad used to take me or whatever and then when they said 'no' it was a big rejection.
> "I was a silk screen printer for all of five weeks. I was a glorified tea-boy really! Then I went to Forest for a game and they asked me to play in their youth team on a Wednesday afternoon. I think I played two games and they asked if I would like to be an apprentice."

His debut for the full England side may have been relatively incident free at a time when 'ordinary' black people were getting abused daily on the street and in the workplace but Anderson was not so fortunate during his Forest career.

The legend that was Brian Clough was pivotal to Anderson's career both on and off the pitch. England in the late 1970s and '80s was a hostile place if you were not white and Clough's famous strength of character did much to shape Anderson as a person and as a player. Anderson's Forest career did not get off to the most auspicious of starts as Clough was intent on stamping his authority on him from the start.

"From day one when he walked in the door he set a standard. I recall we drew with Tottenham at home in the FA Cup and I was only 17 and I came on with ten minutes to go. The replay was on the Wednesday, the team-sheet went up. Cloughie took Tony Woodcock, who was not even in the squad, to the game and we assumed it was because the coaches had said Tony was a good player. As it eventually turned out Cloughie took Tony just to clean his shoes!

"The team was at the dinner table – I wasn't there so this is Tony telling the story – and the squad were all having dinner and Cloughie says to Tony 'Go get my shoes cleaned.'

"Tony started looking at the older players and the older players said he should get on with it – so he did! All he did was fetch and carry for the three days the team were down in London. Tony thought he had a chance of being in the squad or the bench whatever but at the end of it he was just taken to do bits and bobs. That was Cloughie's way of giving players a taste of the first team but balancing that with reality.

"I remember a match soon after and my name wasn't on the team-sheet. I thought the writing is on the wall for me. I thought he didn't fancy me."

Two matches later Anderson was back in Clough's starting XI and the rest is history. The pair enjoyed a mutual respect during the club's glory years.

Viv Anderson's Breakthrough

Clough was known for his hardline approach on player discipline and was always quick to offer advice to his players no matter how unpalatable. Anderson recalls playing away at Carlisle and coming under attack from racists on the terraces and, just as importantly, how Clough dealt with the situation.

"Cloughie says 'Anderson warm up.' So I warm up and I am getting dog's abuse from the crowd. So I sit down very shortly afterwards and he says 'I thought I told you to warm up?' I said 'I have been warming up but they are booing me and all sorts!' He said 'Get up and warm up.' So I had to get up again and do it and from that day on I have just dealt with it.

"Afterwards he did pull me to one side and say 'Listen if you are going to let this sort of thing bother you, you are not going to be in my football club and you are not going to be in my team because it can affect your play on the football field. So at the end of the day you either make a career for yourself or not, because if you let it bother you you are not going to have a career.' So from that day on I just thought 'that's it I'm getting on regardless'.

"Yes, it was literally black or white for Cloughie. He said you do it or you don't do it. If you don't do it, I am going to pick somebody else because he is going to perform better. You are not going to perform to your abilities if you listen to them [the racists]".

One of the opponents he had to face early in his career was Laurie Cunningham, the most gifted player of his generation according to those that played against him or watched him live. A black rival to the equally gifted George Best.

"As a person Laurie was very quiet. At one of my first England games we went to Bulgaria and Laurie was at Real Madrid at the time. We were in the room together and I remember looking at his Mercedes and I was thinking he can afford a Mercedes car! But he was very reserved.

"On the pitch he was a great player and did amazing things with the football. He was really good. He played on the right hand side when we played at West Brom. He had the lot; natural talent, everything you could possibly think of. It was tragic that his life was cut so short so quickly.

"You can never say for sure how big he was going to be. You don't know what could have happened to his career but at that age going to Real Madrid was a big deal. People talk about the David Beckhams and Michael Owens of this world moving to Spain but it was done by Laurie twenty odd years beforehand so you have got to think of him as a really good player."

Cunningham was what black players were supposed to be, quick and skilful. Anderson was an uncompromising full-back. The cynics who suggested that black players were not up for a fight, or tackle, thus making them a liability, were confounded by the Nottingham Forest right-back. The hundreds of black players who have come through since have, in the main, been midfield players and forwards who grab the glory and headlines. For the man who still has difficulty appreciating that he made history, the progress of black footballers was always on the cards.

"I think it is a natural progression definitely, because obviously there were not many black players at the time. I have said loads of times there was only Clyde Best that I could relate to and then I came along.

"There was Brendon Batson who was a little bit older than me, then I came along, Cyrille came along. I think it is just a natural progression now. There were not many black faces in football clubs. Now if you go to most clubs you find they have all got black players and lots of them, so it was always natural what was going to follow.

"It is a multi-cultural society really now so it can only get bigger and better. The only surprising thing is that there are no Asians coming to the fore. I think that is the next stage. I don't know why it hasn't happened yet. I don't know if their parents bring them up to do other things. Or school is more important I don't know but I think it will happen eventually.

"I know that Michael Chopra is doing a little bit better than most. He was among the first of the Asian players to break through and everyone thought he was going to be the one that was going to be the genuine article. He didn't live up to his potential but I think that the next stage for football is an influx of Asian players. I think as there are so many Asian people living in England now and they love football. When you go to these places they know more about my career than I do myself but they need someone to come along and break the mould."

In 1997, Anderson was voted Nottingham Forest's best-ever right-back by the club's fans, polling a staggering 96% of the votes, no surprise really as he had helped the club to two European Cups.

After the Forest fairytale, Arsenal were Anderson's

next employers. He made his debut at home to Chelsea on the opening day of the 1984-85 season. At Highbury he cemented his reputation as a swashbuckling right-back with an eye for goal with 15 strikes in 150 appearances for the North London club. Anderson was to play a significant part in the development of future Highbury stars during his spell in North London.

He mentored a young Tony Adams and he also helped the Gunners to the 1987 League Cup, their first trophy under George Graham.

Anderson must have liked Scottish managers because at the start of the 1987-88 season he joined Alex Ferguson's Manchester United for £250,000. Once again he proved to be a solid performer during his four seasons at Old Trafford.

After four seasons with Ferguson's Red Devils, Anderson joined Sheffield Wednesday where he made nearly one hundred league appearances and helped them to promotion to the First Division. In 1993 he left to join neighbours Barnsley as manager before joining his old United teammate Brian Robson as assistant manager at Middlesbrough.

Anderson clearly has a penchant for writing history. Having been the first to don the senior England jersey, his sortie into management was one of the first by a black coach.

Having played under the likes of Bobby Robson, Clough, Ron Atkinson and George Graham, Anderson had a more than decent foundation to his track suit days.

"I think I took a bit of something from all of them. I was privileged to work with Bobby Robson and Alex Ferguson and Big Ron. But at the end of the day you have got to have your own style in management. I tried to form my own views and my own ideas of doing things because I didn't want to be a clone of Brian Clough or Alex Ferguson or whoever. I wanted to be myself.

"Not many black players move into the management side. That surprises me and I don't know what the reason is. If you talk about Luther Blissett, he is more qualified than most. He has been in the game a long time and been at different levels. John Barnes is the same.

"There are not that many opportunities. I was very fortunate because I came out with a year's contract at Barnsley and out of courtesy I spoke to the Barnsley chairman and he convinced me that it was the right thing to do. To become a player-manager is a hard job because you are combining the two things.

"I enjoyed my year and the only reason I went to Middlesbrough is because Brian Robson and the chairman sold it to me. Brian is still a dear friend and I knew what was required because I was still playing. I was to do virtually what I had been doing at Barnsley. I would virtually be running the team. I had a say and that was crucial for me. The only reason why I went was because I had a say in everything. Buying, selling, who we got rid of, everything. I was part of every aspect of running a football club, that is the only reason I would have gone. I had eight great years."

The modest Anderson describes his exit from The Riverside thus:

"At the end of the day we just did our time. Peter Reid did a similar sort of time for Sunderland. If the players hear the same voices and hear the same things for too long it is time for a change."

While many former players complain bitterly of lack of opportunity, Anderson is not one of them. He has been given opportunity and grasped it.

"Inevitably, not many managers hang around for eight years. Alex Ferguson is an exception because he has won eighteen trophies in the twenty years, or something like that. There are not many of those managers about, so I felt it was time to move on. The opportunities after that have been few and far between. I could have done various jobs but I wasn't really convinced. I have enjoyed my time in football but I have got my own company now.

"I am disappointed that there aren't many black faces involved in the top end of football. There are a lot of them at the bottom end. There are lots of black players now and everything else but it is on the coaching side and the management side that we have to bridge the gap.

"I think we have the people to do it. Look at the Paul Inces of this world. You would think Paul Ince would be the next obvious one to get a coaching/management position but he has got to get the opportunity.

"He has lots of money and has done well for himself, now whether he will get the opportunity at the top end I don't know, because invariably now clubs are going for foreign coaches. It's in vogue at the moment and everybody has gone foreign. It makes it more restricting for a black British person to get in.

"I loved my time in management. It was hard like everything else but I got paid a lot of money to make hard decisions, difficult decisions. That is part of being management.

Viv Anderson's Breakthrough

"My colour was never an issue. Not at all. The supporters remember what you did as a player. At one Luton game I got some stick but because you stand up all the time you are in the forefront. You are an easy target."

Anderson is hopeful that his son Charlie, at Macclesfield's academy, can benefit from his father's experience.

"I never go and watch the coaching. I watch the games. I let them get on with it because it might not be helpful if I stood around watching him with a critical eye. But all they say to me is that he loves what he does and he has a smile on his face and is a credit to the club and the team. So I think that is good but at the end of the day it has got to be about ability. You can smile as much as you like but has he got the ability to make it? You never know do you? I hope he does because he likes it so much."

Even though he had a famous tackle, Anderson, courtesy of quality legs that would snare the ball, played the game in the right spirit. He may not have always had a smile on his face but he was mindful that whenever he was playing he should enjoy the experience while learning his trade.

"Yes, enjoy what you do. If you are going to get involved and worry about things, such as whether you are going to get picked, it is inevitable you won't be successful. It drives you to do well for yourself. Now it comes out in different forms in different people. I used to work really hard because I had a bad knee but football gives you a discipline from an early age.

"I did my knee when I was seventeen so I had to go in half-an-hour before anybody else to make sure the knee was right so I could perform on a Saturday afternoon. It gave me a regime – I just had to do it. Even to this day I still do it. I might go out for a jog or I will go to the gym to make sure I look after the knee. And that is what football, and Cloughie especially, gave me. It gave me a discipline in life that you do things correctly and the best way you can.

"I think it is good for young lads to get involved in the sport because it does give you a good basis. My lad has got to be at the club at a certain time. He has got to turn up, he has got to have his kit, he has to have this, that and the other and that hopefully will take him throughout his life."

Listening to Anderson talk about attitude and discipline shows just how much black players have developed. Many of them were seen as the soft centre of teams because of a so-called lack of these two traits.

"It is not just football, you can use it in life in general. If I have a meeting for example. If my appointment turns up at twelve o'clock and I turn up at half past twelve that is not acceptable. They may have come all the way from London to Manchester to see me so the least I can do is make sure that I am on time. But what they don't know is that I got in at four o'clock that morning and I made sure I was there. That's the professional thing to do.

"You have to listen and learn from your peers. I was lucky that I had the likes of Frank Clark around me. I learnt from a lot of people. I was lucky I had a good manager early on. I had Dave

McKay when I was an apprentice. He was only there for a year and I learnt a hell of a lot from him in a short space of time. So I was lucky to come along and get in touch with a lot of world-renowned names. I grew up with these people and I was very, very fortunate. The best thing is to listen and learn."

Chapter 6

The Three Degrees

WEST BROMWICH ALBION was an impressive source of inspiration for young black players and no history of black players in the English game would be complete without mention of the 'Three Degrees'. Ron Atkinson's side included three black stars in the regular first team line-up; Laurie Cunningham, Brendon Batson and Cyrille Regis. This development was seen by many commentators as a pioneering and bold move at a time when many clubs had no black players and racial stereotyping was common in coaching and managerial circles.

Regis broke into the first team within a few months of signing for West Brom in May 1977 and remembers the racial abuse that he endured initially from some of the Hawthorns crowd: "I think they were rebelling against me 'cause I'd taken a white guy's place in the team".

However, the West Brom fans, impressed by his early scoring exploits, were quickly to warm to the former electrician who joined from non-league Hayes. Regis believed that it was this early recognition and acceptance of his talents by the club and fans alike which allowed his career at West Brom to develop. Members of large black communities in nearby Handsworth also provided some active support for Regis and his colleagues at a time when black fans were reluctant to attend matches for fear of their own safety. Regis would later reach the pinnacle of his career in 1987, when he was a key figure in Coventry City's FA Cup winning triumph.

West Brom's famous 'Three Degrees' did more than most to promote the merits of the black footballer. Watson, Wharton, Tull, Johanneson, Best and Podd attempted to perform without any friendly faces to turn to when things inevitably went wrong.

Cunningham, Regis and Batson were to become a small but powerful collective. They proved to be the heartbeat of not only the team but also the club.

Jokingly named by manager Atkinson after the hit pop divas of the 1970s, the three West Brom players did as much for manager Ron Atkinson as they did for their own careers. The manager trusted his Three Degrees and seemingly made it acceptable to put black players regularly in a professional starting XI.

In a BBC Radio 4 tribute to the trio, *Three Degrees West: The Story of Three Pioneer Footballers*, Regis recalled: "It was radical. West Brom was a focal point of a serious change in black football having three black players who were breaking down serious barriers."

Atkinson, whose selection of the three was considered radical at the time but is totally normal in today's multi-national game, said: "They had great attitude and ability... it doesn't matter what colour you are, it's who you are that counts".

All three brought something different to the mix but there is no doubt that Cunningham was the first true modern black British superstar.

He first made his name at Leyton Orient with a string of pacy, goal-getting displays, and went on to play for ten different clubs in four countries.

West Brom were next on his list of employers and it was while at the Hawthorns that Cunningham took the First Division by storm. With Cunningham pulling the strings and providing the goals for Cyrille Regis, Albion were to become one of the most attractive and exciting English sides.

Cunningham became the first black player to wear an England shirt at any level in the modern era when playing, and scoring, in an under-21 friendly against Scotland in April 1977. Amazingly, for a player blessed with so much talent, he gained only six caps for the senior national side.

In 1979 he moved to Real Madrid for £5000 short of £1million, winning a championship medal and two cup winners' medals. Cunningham was loaned to Manchester United in 1983 in a bid to revive a career that was beginning to flag. Old Trafford was followed by a move to Leicester City before transfers to foreign fields; a return to Spain with Sporting Gijon and then Charleroi of Belgium.

He was to return to the English game with unfashionable Wimbledon at the start of the 1987-88 season. Although his first team opportunities with the so-called Crazy Gang were limited, he made a substitute appearance in one of the biggest FA Cup Final upsets of all time when Wimbledon beat the mighty Liverpool 1-0 in 1988. Soon after that Cunningham made yet another move to Spain, this time signing for Rayo Vallecano.

On the morning of 15 July, 1989, Cunningham was killed in a car crash at the age of 33. His contribution to the promotion of black footballers, however, lives on to this very day as the silky skills he displayed are replicated by the world's top soccer players.

Regis, too, left his mark. Off the field this hustling, bustling powerhouse of a centre-forward is one of the most personable, softly spoken individuals you could wish to meet.

The Three Degrees

John Fashanu, Ian Wright and Emile Heskey have all adopted something from the Regis game in terms of physicality and aggression.

Regis and the other two degrees broke down, under the watchful eye of increased media and TV coverage, the mythology and prejudice that black players could not hack the rigours of English football.

"They said if Cyrille Regis can do it, I can do it. So retrospectively, we can say we had an impact on black boys in this country," said Regis himself on the BBC Radio 4 tribute.

The powerful footballing physique and mental determination of Regis earned him numerous nicknames, including the most apt, 'Smokin' Joe', in reference to former heavyweight boxing champion Joe Frazier.

Regis gives an insight into his family's history on his official website:

> "My father Robert originated from the picturesque island of St Lucia. He eventually moved ... married my mum Mathilde, aka Gladys.Between 1962 and 1963 mum and dad embarked on a new journey to England. My father travelled to England on his own to set up a home so the rest of us could join him in London. My sister Nila, brother Imbert and I had to learn quickly to adjust to the harsh climate and realities of a British way of life in the sixties. A few years later the family was complete with the arrival of my younger sister Denise and my brother David, who went on to play for Notts County.
>
> "Moving from primary school in Kensal Rise to secondary school in Harlesden, opened up a whole range of sport that I couldn't wait to get involved with, but football of course was at the

heart of all my energy. The game became a passion in my life that I never thought would provide me with a career and so many enjoyable memories.

"I spent many great years playing non-league and Sunday league football within the Regents Park and Barnet Sunday Leagues, moving on to play for Molesey FC and Hayes FC in the Isthmian League. At the same time I was training to be an electrician.

"Just as I had formally qualified and completed my City & Guilds training, I was spotted by West Bromwich Albion scout Ronnie Allen, who was instrumental in me signing my first professional playing contract with WBA in 1977."

Regis went on to play 297 times for his beloved Albion. He then had spells with Coventry City, Aston Villa, Wolverhampton Wanderers, Wycombe Wanderers and Chester City. In more than 700 appearances he registered 205 goals.

He will always be remembered for his physical stature, explosive pace and goals and was a catalyst for the many great black goal scorers. Ian Wright freely discloses that Regis was his hero.

The death of Cunningham was to change how Regis saw life. It put things into perspective. "Two years before Laurie died, he and I were involved in a similar crash, but we walked away with our lives intact."

His developing relationship with Jesus saw Regis become a born-again Christian, renewing his mind and changing his behaviour according to God's word.

Now Regis, who has turned his hand to the role of football agent/advisor, is more than happy to promote the merits of footballers.

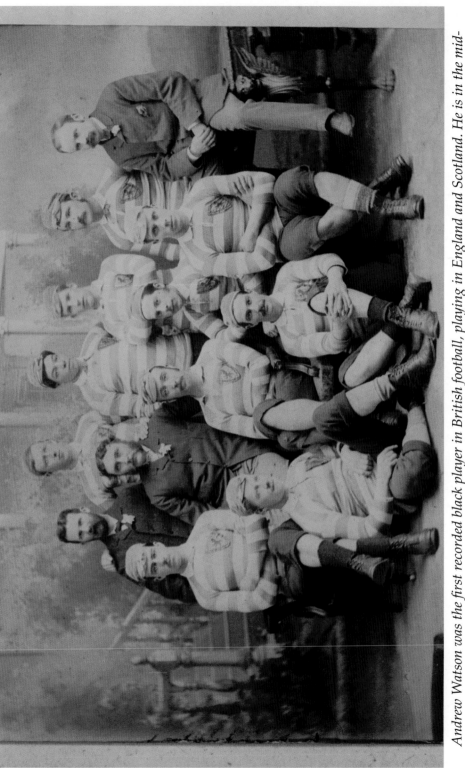

Andrew Watson was the first recorded black player in British football, playing in England and Scotland. He is in the middle of the back row of the Scottish team that played England in 1882. (Scottish Football Museum).

Arthur Wharton was the first black professional player in England in the 1880s. He played for, among others, Preston North End, Rotherham and Sheffield United as a goalkeeper.

Walter Tull played for Tottenham and Northampton but was killed in the first World War. (Haringey Museum)

One of the few black players in the 1950s was Charlie Williams of Doncaster, seen here with goalkeeper Harry Gregg and Leyton Orient's Tom Johnston. Williams went on to TV fame as a comedian and presenter.

Albert Johanneson was arguably the most famous black player in the 1960s, starring on the left wing for Leeds United.

Mike Trebilcock became the first black player in an FA Cup final when his two goals helped Everton beat Sheffield Wednesday 3-2 in 1966.

Clyde Best was a powerful role model for many black youngsters when he played up front for West Ham United.

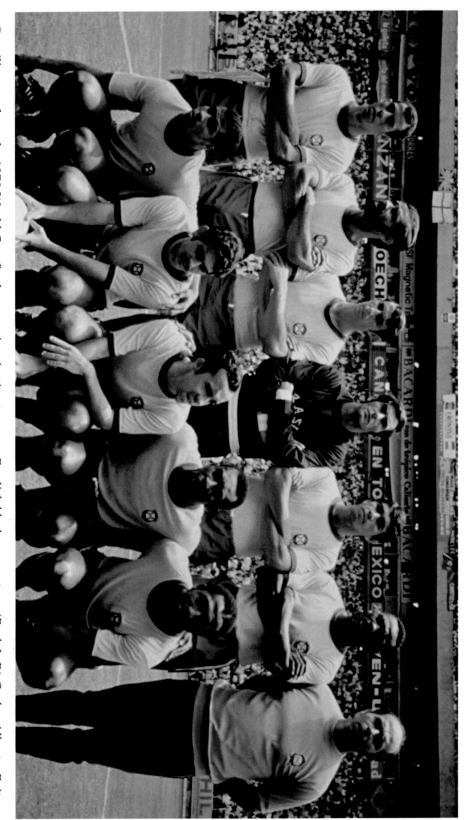

Brazil's team from the 1970 World Cup final was an inspiration to many English black youngsters. (Back L–R) Carlos Alberto, Brito, Wilson Piazza, Felix, Clodoaldo, Everaldo, Mario Zagalo. (Front L–R) Jairzinho, Tostao, Pele, Paulo Cesar.

Ces Podd made 565 appearances for Bradford City

Laurie Cunningham was one of the most gifted players of his generation and the first black player to wear an England shirt in the modern era when he played for the Under 21s in 1977.

Cunningham played with Cyrille Regis at West Bromwich Albion and went on to win an FA Cup winners' medal with Coventry City.

Brendon Batson (pictured with Sir Trevor Brooking) was one of the "Three Degrees"
at West Brom. He went on to have a distinguished administrative career with the
Professional Footballers' Association, the Football Association and his old club.

Garth Crooks, seen with his wife Funkazi after receiving an OBE for services to the Institute of Professional Sport in 1999, was a star striker with Stoke City and Tottenham Hotspur. He is now a broadcaster with the BBC.

Viv Anderson became the first black player to represent the full England team when he played against Czechoslovakia in 1978. He had a distinguished career as a full back for Nottingham Forest, Arsenal and Manchester United.

Justin Fashanu became the first black player to command a £1m fee when he joined Nottingham Forest from Norwich City. He later took his own life.

Justin Fashanu's younger brother John became a formidable centre forward with England, Wimbledon and Aston Villa. Later he moved into TV.

"My mission is to portray a positive view of life as a black footballer, not excluding the harsh realities of racism that still rears its head."

Batson may not have had the same eye-catching career as Cunningham and Regis but his contribution to football has been equally immense.

Born in St Georges, Grenada in 1953, the Batson family moved to England when Brendon was just nine. Before then, he had never even watched a game of football.

However, he was signed as a schoolboy by Arsenal, and was the first black player to play for the Gunners. Competition for places at Highbury was intense and Batson failed to stave off the challenge to gain the right-back berth. In his way were international full-backs like Pat Rice, Sammy Nelson and Bob McNab who all became regulars for Arsenal.

Batson was to make just ten appearances for the red and white half of north London before he moved to Cambridge United. It was while at United that Batson was to meet and strike up a strong friendship with Ron Atkinson.

United were to become a force which put the larger-than-life Atkinson in the management shop window. He caught the eye of West Bromwich Albion's direc-tors in 1978 inheriting a team that already included youth team graduate Bryan Robson. Cunningham and Regis were also there, having been bought at bargain prices from the lower divisions. On his appointment as manager he went back to Cambridge to acquire the services of Batson for just £30,000.

The right-back went on to form part of West Brom's underrated backline which included Derek Statham, John Wile and Ally Robertson. While Cunningham and Regis grabbed the headlines, Batson and his fellow defenders just got on with the task of keeping out the opposition.

While the other two degrees were rewarded for their club efforts with full England recognition, Batson was not so fortunate. He never won a full England cap even though he played more than 172 times for WBA.

A serious injury sustained at Ipswich Town in October 1982 was the beginning of the end of Batson's career. Many consider that the timing of his injury was a significant factor in the decline of West Brom's champagne football style. A great team, which played the game the right way, was on the verge of breaking up.

Batson was finally forced to retire from playing in 1984 but another football door opened quickly when the Professional Footballers' Association's chief executive Gordon Taylor asked him to become his assistant.

Batson accepted and had a wide ranging portfolio, playing a tireless role in the development of the Football in the Community programme, and with the PFA's work in attempting to kick racism out of the game. Whether he was taking up disciplinary issues on behalf of members or advising them on financial matters and their futures, Batson has always gone about his work with the calm assurance of a man in control.

During his tenure as deputy chief executive the PFA became a multi-million pound operation and one of the richest trade unions in the world.

He left the PFA to return to WBA in 2002 after they gained Premiership status. Everyone at the PFA was sad to see him go and he left with the best wishes of all he had worked with and with the heartfelt thanks of chief executive Taylor. He said at the time: "It is with great regret that we are losing the services of such a valuable member of the PFA team because Brendon's contribution over the last twenty years has been immense, not least in his capacity as my very able deputy.

"I would personally like to extend my thanks to him for all he has done on behalf of this organisation over the last couple of decades and I wish him well at his new career at The Hawthorns. The PFA's loss is certainly West Brom's gain."

However, the love affair between West Brom and Batson lost its passion shortly afterwards and Batson left to take up a Project Manager's post at the Football Association.

Chapter 7

Luther Blissett

LUTHER BLISSETT FOLLOWED Cyrille Regis into the England side and what an impact he was to make. He became the first black player to score for England when he claimed a hat-trick against Luxembourg, his first full appearance.

While Laurie Cunningham's glamorous transfer to Real Madrid was just reward for a player with silky skills, Luther Blissett's transfer to AC Milan in the summer of 1983 shocked the football world and Blissett himself.

Blissett's move to the Italian giants came as a reward for prolific scoring and that hat-trick for England. The cordial forward, during his hot streak in the late 1970s to early '80s, proved that all things are possible. In his first spell at Watford, between 1975 and 1983, he scored 95 League goals in just 246 appearances, thereby establishing himself as one of the most prolific strikers in the British game.

Three times a Watford player, he still holds the club record at Vicarage Road for both the amount of appearances (415) and goals (158).

He is the first to admit that without the support of his mother Gloria and the rest of his family he may not have been able to complete his fairytale career.

"The overwhelming thing is that football was what I wanted to do. I wanted to achieve. I thank my mother for giving me the opportunity to pursue something that I really wanted to do. She did everything to encourage me. She couldn't drive so she could never take me to games while dad was working.

"I had to get to places by bus and train, which was the only way to travel – or walk. You learnt the independent things. You also learnt that the worse thing you can ever do is not try."

Blissett was certainly a trier. He did not have the skill of Cunningham but he did have pace and was brave. One of his early heroes was Manchester United legend George Best.

While Blissett lacked Best's twinkled-toed talents he gave everything for the cause. Watford and England were to be the beneficiaries of his endeavour.

Recalling his early days watching the game, Blissett speaks fondly of Best.

"I met him for the first time in 2004 and I just had to tell him that I was pleased to meet him. It wasn't anything to do with the way he conducted himself off the field but it was totally and absolutely what he did with a football and just watching him do what he did.

"Obviously Pele and other players from that time just reinforced even more why I wanted to play football. I said to myself 'I would love to be able to walk out there and do some of the things that these guys do.'"

It was when he was urged to join a school friend to go to Watford for training at the age of 15 that things really began to take off for Blissett. Ironically that first training session was held at RAF Stanmore, just a stone's throw from the family home in Harlesden in north-west London.

Blissett recalls:

"I was told to bring my trainers and just join in, so I did. Six other guys and I went and it just started from there. I had never done training before. They started with things like fitness training, weights and circuits. I was thinking 'what has this got to do with football?' It was totally foreign to me. It was that session which first opened my eyes. It was something totally different to what I had been doing since I took up football.

"I'd never worked so hard. I had never done anything like it apart from cross-country running at school. What we used to do then was start running but as soon as we were out of sight of the teachers we would walk. That was as much training that I ever did.

"I hated running, but give me a ball and I could run all day with that." Even though he found the going tough, Blissett's tenacity and traditional West Indian family values of perseverance and hard work made him ride the culture shock.

Two goals in a 3-1 win against Southend's under-17 side guaranteed Blissett a contract with Watford, and a career that was to be graced with an equal number of highs and lows was now under way.

Ron Atkinson may have been famous for the 'Three Degrees' but in a less flamboyant way Graham Taylor, later to manage England, was equally instrumental in the development of black players in the Football League. He had played a major role in Blissett's career and also that of another Watford starlet, John Barnes.

Luckily for Blissett, his signing with Watford dovetailed neatly with the appointment of Taylor at the Hertfordshire club. The two, alongside celebrity chairman and fan Elton John, were to help put Watford on the football map as well as put to bed some of the negatives surrounding black players.

Blissett was to become a crucial member of Taylor's Watford side which rose up through the lower ranks of English football, to finish second to Liverpool in the 1982-83 championship race. In that season, the newly-promoted Hornets took everybody by surprise with their direct style of play and Blissett's eye for a goal.

"He [Taylor] had a meeting with all the professionals, face to face, when he came to the club. I met him in his office and his first words to me were, and he said my name about twice, 'With a name like that you have got to be a star!' And that was where it all started.

> "For the first season that he was there I was on the subs bench almost all season. There was only one substitute at the time so he would use me, because being really quick I was somebody good to throw on especially at the latter stage of the game when the opposition were tiring. You could stick the ball over the top of them and they didn't want to chase me because they weren't going to catch me anyway.
>
> "It worked very well for us that season. And at the end of that season I remember him saying to me, because by then I would have been coming on nineteen, 'It is time now, you have had a season on the bench it is now about time you started making a name for yourself and stay in the team.'
>
> "He saw something in me and he said just to keep working at things, to be consistent. He said if I got in the team and made a place then nobody would get me out. And so it proved actually."

Black Lions

Watford's Vicarage Road ground proved to be a safe haven for Blissett, by now a key member of the playing staff. While his pace – stereotypes again – was of value to his team, his colour was proving to be an issue with the bigots who supported Watford's opponents.

"My colour was never an issue within the actual football club. There would be a lot of comments about colour and all that sort of thing but my attitude to it was 'sticks and stones'. You know 'call me whatever names you like' but at the end of the day that is all it is, just calling me a name.

"That was never ever going to hurt me. It might upset me for a bit but it is never really going to hurt me. That was my attitude towards it so it never became an issue at the club.

"You would take no notice most of the time of the things people would say to you; you just got on with what you were doing. One thing I soon realised is that you can't fight with everybody if they call you names.

"That is one sure way of ending a career even before it has begun. So it was a case of getting my head down and showing people; answering people back by what I did out on the field. This sort of thing went on especially when we played away from home. I got that abuse. I got it from players, the opposition want to do it to you to upset you and you got it from the opposition fans everywhere you went. The first time it happened for me in a crowd of people would have been at a reserve game at Peterborough and I was absolutely shocked.

"I thought to myself 'what is all this about?' That is when I found out my teammates were very good people. They would say 'Don't worry about it.'

Luther Blissett

They would always say, 'Stick the ball in the net, that will shut the bastards up.' That sort of thing allowed you to get on with your game.

"That sort of abuse I got everywhere I went for the next two or three years. It slowly got less and less because as they couldn't upset me by it, and because they couldn't put me off my game it became a case of they didn't bother any more. Obviously more and more black players were playing and more and more clubs had them so it was a case that the clubs themselves were telling their players 'You can't be abusing the opposition's black players because don't forget you have got black players on your team as well.'"

As one of the early black football pioneers his contribution may not have been truly recognised but it was massive.

Blissett's experiences while playing for Watford were to stand him in good stead for the barbs that followed his move to Milan and when he played for England. In his first spell at Watford, between 1975 and 1983, Blissett, born in Falmouth, Jamaica, scored his near century of league goals to establish himself as one of the most prolific strikers, black or white, in the game. He is still revered in the Hertfordshire area.

Oddly his name is recognised not just in football circles. 'Luther Blissett' became the name of an Italian anarchist society and is associated with general anti-establishment behaviour. In 1997 four men went on trial in Rome for travelling on a train without tickets. When asked to identify themselves, all they said was 'Luther Blissett' and argued that as a collective identity, they did not need a ticket!

As Taylor's side were putting noses out of joint with their route one style of play, Blissett's goals, alongside the gangly Ross Jenkins, were getting the club noticed. His two televised goals in 1978 in a League Cup tie against Manchester United at Old Trafford gained him a reputation but that brace was nothing compared to the adulation he received with twenty-seven goals, including four in one game in an 8-0 destruction of Sunderland, during their pursuit of Liverpool in 1982/83. The annihilation of Sunderland saw Blissett score Watford's third, fifth, seventh and eighth goals in what was only his and his team's seventh appearance in football's top division.

One of the most likeable and genial men in football, Blissett was now at the top of his game. Inevitably an England cap beckoned.

England manager Bobby Robson was the man who bestowed international honours on Blissett – who must have needed a helmet at this time, his career was moving so dangerously fast. Blissett won the first of his fourteen caps when he came on as substitute in a 2-1 defeat to West Germany at Wembley.

Viv Anderson might have been the first black player to play for the senior side in 1978 but Blissett was to make just as powerful an impact in a shirt adorned with Three Lions when in his first England start in December 1983, he bagged a hat-trick against the minnows of Luxembourg, a game that ended 9-0 in front of a thrilled Wembley, a game which this writer was privileged to witness from the press box.

While Blissett's England career was at its apex, off the field it was a time for quiet contemplation. Playing for your national side, no matter what colour you are, is the ultimate honour but Blissett felt more than a little removed from the whole international set-up despite the fact that he was the man of the moment.

"Because I was from a lower league club playing with First Division players, I never really felt a real part of it. Whilst I was there I got on with it and I was friendly with one or two people which was good, but I never actually felt a big part of it because they were so far removed from me.

"You don't really feel a part of the set-up especially initially when you always feel that you are on the outside of this sort of club. You play a few games here and there, and people may think that I am a bit blasé, but the biggest thing about playing for England was being called up to play.

"After that for me it was just a football match. Say what you like or maybe it's the way that I dealt with it. All that hype and everything, it just boiled down to me putting on my boots and going out there and playing. That is how I treated every professional football match no matter who I was playing against."

Even though Blissett scored a hat-trick against Luxembourg, some of the media preferred to dwell on the goal chances he had missed. It may be too easy, even churlish, to say the critics rounded on the Watford man because of his colour but he more than understood that playing for England bought a different pressure for a black player no matter what exalted heights he hit at club level.

"The media started panning me by saying I could have had six goals instead of three, which is stating the obvious for any striker in any match. However, it's a rarity if any striker takes all his chances in a match just as it's a rarity when a striker misses all his chances.

"Maybe I got the stick because of the club that I was playing for. If you look at things a little bit wider I felt people like Andrew Cole and Ian Wright, especially Wrighty, never got the real sort of accolades or whatever for playing for England that he should have done.

"You've got to give people time at international level but they were never given any time. I like Alan Shearer but Alan Shearer went through a period of time when he was not scoring for England but he kept going. Why? They believed that he would do it. And sometimes certain players are not afforded that same sort of leeway. I think that is not necessarily right."

Blissett, Cyrille Regis, Les Ferdinand, Wright and Cole were expected to perform miracles from the first whistle to the last in an England shirt. The former Watford man knows the simple reason why that is. Are black players under more scrutiny, thus increased pressure?

"Of course they are. The big reason is you stand out more. For a start, a little analogy. You hear comments from media pundits when they are doing football matches in which players are wearing, say, white boots. And they say 'you had better play well today wearing those.' Why? Because, simply, every time the player with white boots does anything people will notice the boots. That is what it boils down to.

"So if he makes a mistake they say it is the boots doing it. It is no different to a black player because they will notice him all the time. He may wear the same strip as his teammates but he is the only black face out there. So people notice everything he does all the time. Whereas when you are just another white face you can get away with more in a group than you can do if you stand out of that group."

While Blissett was immensely proud to play for his adopted country, as all the black players to have represented the Three Lions have been, he still was not prepared for the hate mail and verbal abuse he was to suffer while playing for England. Quite literally he went from hero to zero. While he was giving his all for England, some of the country's racists were using the national sport to let Blissett and other black footballers know that whatever their deeds on the field they would never truly be accepted.

Blissett never gave them the satisfaction of win-ning their racist argument.

"It was no different to the stuff that I got when I played league football. I got it, read it, had a little chuckle, then binned it. That was it.

"The press would make comments making your colour a big part of their story so you weren't going to get any support in that respect and within football itself it was always a case of if you said anything you were supposed to have got a chip on your shoulder.

"I made sure I avoided that scenario so they couldn't ever throw that at me about having a chip on my shoulder. I got my head down and got on with it. Whatever people threw at me, I put a smile on my face. I ran out there and I really just let them know without shouting and hollering that I was better than they were. You can deal with that, do your job and still laugh in their faces. That was the kind of attitude I had.

"There was no other way really. Because if I went out there shouting my mouth off what I said would have been turned around and used against me. Then it would have been a case of the 'chip on the shoulder thing' and bleating about this and that. So it had to be done and it was one of those times when it had to be done just by reaction. And what I had to do was play and produce my best every time. You had to let your football do the talking. But now players can actually come out, there is a platform for them."

Blissett's only solace was the camaraderie he built up with the likes of Kenny Sansom and Billy Gilbert and the few black players who were also coming through at the time, such as Stoke City's Mark Chamberlain, Manchester City goalkeeper Alex Williams, Cyrille Regis and Crystal Palace winger Vince Hillaire.

Despite the reputation of Watford as a family club, Blissett's club and international form saw him swap Watford's homely Vicarage Road ground for the grandeur of the San Siro stadium, home of AC and Inter Milan. When AC came calling in 1983 it was one of the most surprise transfers in football history.

The stories regarding Blissett's move to AC are many and contradictory, with many cynics suggesting that Milan signed the wrong player from England – the Milan giants wanting John Barnes' services and not those of Blissett. There has been many a time when the saying 'all blacks look alike' has been suggested for Blissett's move to Milan, a classic case of 'they all look the same.'

Blissett's record of just five goals in thirty appearances in Italy suggests it was not a marriage made in heaven but the fact remains that prior to joining the Italian aristocrats, Blissett had struck 27 goals in one season for his club and in December 1983 he had recorded the first England hat-trick by a black player. The transfer from the Hornets and homely Vicarage Road to the palatial San Siro has often been listed among the worst ten football signings but the fact that on his return from Italy Blissett bagged twenty-one goals indicates that while his up-and-at-them style might not have been to some purists' tastes he certainly knew where the goal was.

Having endured racist abuse aplenty in his adopted country while playing for the national side, Blissett was certainly asking for potential trouble with a move to Italy, a country known to have more than enough racists of its own. But ever the optimist, Blissett took up the biggest challenge of his professional career when he signed for Milan for £1million.

"I enjoyed the Italian experience because it was a challenge. A challenge never worries me, but nobody likes failing, for want of a better word. And not scoring the number of goals that I had been used to scoring was failure to me.

"It made it doubly hard because the expectation was massive. You have got 60,000, 70,000, 80,000 people there who want to see their team do well at home. And the team was not a patch on the team that was there three or four years previously which made it very difficult. But I enjoyed it because it taught me a lot of things.

"It reinforced certain things, such as you had to get your head down and work hard at what you were doing. I went through some rough times and I had got the press on my back. It wasn't so much the press out in Italy but the press in England, which didn't support me in any way. It makes you almost want to write another story on the back of what happened to me out in Italy. The criticism I took in England was not the way things should have been done."

Blissett was transferred back to Vicarage Road for half of what he cost. He enjoyed the return and the goals started flowing freely once more. But life with England was never quite the same. His twelve appearances for the national side after his Italian adventure produced no goals, just a hammering from the press who dubbed him 'Luther Miss It'. His last England cap came in June 1984, a 2-0 defeat by the USSR.

His sojourn with Watford ended briefly in 1988 when he joined Bournemouth, only for another move to Watford in 1991 before he ended his professional career with moves to West Brom, Bury and Mansfield Town.

Having worked so hard to make a name for himself as a footballer, Blissett, after hanging up his boots, has found successfully breaking into management to be yet another test of his patience and mental fortitude.

While coaching or management has always been considered a natural step once a player has retired, it has rarely been the case for black footballers. To this day it is almost impossible for a black player to leave the dressing room and move straight into the manager's chair.

In the spring of 2005 he was disillusioned at the lack of opportunity in management. Managers like Steve Bruce, Steve Coppell, Gordon Strachan and Peter Reid have seen jobs come and go but for the likes of Blissett, and other coaches, there would appear to be a glass ceiling.

"Over the last couple of years I have been frustrated. You do get disillusioned with things because you send off your CV and more times than not you

do not get a reply. And some replies you do get
are a case of 'we will let you know in the next ...'.
When you get one of those letters you know they
are not going to write to you again.
"It is frustrating. I was brought up to believe that
there is a procedure you go through with things.
You would expect professional clubs to have
professional people running them, so you would
think they would at least have the decency to
write back and say thanks for your application
or no thank you. Stick a letter in the post anyway.
They can't even be bothered to do that. How do
you know if they have even bothered to read your
CV, to read what you are about?"

He has advice for some of the clubs which reject out
of hand an application from a black manager.

"The first thing they should look at is are they
qualified to do the job? If they are qualified then
they can see what the applicant has done within
the business. And surely that helps to reinforce
your qualifications. They shouldn't look at your
qualifications and then say that because he has
been an assistant manager and looked after a
reserves team he has never actually managed.
"How can you dismiss somebody on that basis?
Managers have to start somewhere and that
usually means with the youth team or the reserves.
Only the biggest names go straight into it."

Such has been the lack of opportunity in the English
game that Blissett, a thoughtful and articulate football
man, has had to look at possibly coaching one of the
many Caribbean teams, the sort that possess raw
talent but not the same professional acumen of the
game in England.

That said, he believes that in much the same way that black footballers took their punishment and still managed to come up trumps the same will happen with black managers and coaches. One of the present big name players will reap the benefit of work by pioneers such as Blissett.

Dutch legend Ruud Gullit brought success to Chelsea in the 1990s. When he took over at Stamford Bridge, Gullit became the first black manager in the Premier League. But the breakthrough will only truly be made for black managers and coaches in England when a 'name' British player picks up the mantle that was snatched so crudely from the hand of John Barnes at Celtic.

Blissett adds:

"There will be a breakthrough. I think that in many ways we follow America for so many things. In America they had a lot of problems with players in baseball, basketball and that sort of thing. The black players progressed and eventually they are now some of the biggest earners in all those sports.

"And you now see black coaches in basketball, baseball and American Football and in all the major sports. They are accepted now. The attitude over there now seems to be that they can play so they can coach. We have now seen a black owner of an American Football team, and there is no bigger game in America than American Football.

"I think if things keep going the way they have done over here things will improve for black managers and coaches. I would like to be part of it, but I have to ask how long will it take to happen? I think the one thing that will accelerate it will be if one of the big names who are playing now was to say 'I want that job'. They would have a good chance maybe of getting it now. If you got somebody like Sol Campbell, Rio Ferdinand, Thierry Henry wanting to be a manager."

As the 2005-06 season got under way only three black managers were managing and they were certainly not dining at football's top table. Keith Alexander (Lincoln City, now with Peterborough), Carlton Palmer (Mansfield Town) and Leroy Rosenior (Torquay United) were the men entrusted by their respective chairmen to act as the clubs' figureheads. Three men out of a potential ninety-two proves that for all the progress that has been flagged up by the Football Association and the Kick Racism out of Football campaign, the so-called level playing field remains full of potholes for black managers.

Rosenior left Torquay by mutual consent in March 2006 to join Brentford a few months later.

Chapter 8

Growing up in Stoke

WHILE THE NUMBER of black footballers playing in the Football League was steadily increasing – there were about fifty black professionals in the late 1970s – so too was the level of racist activity organised by far-right wing groups in and around many football stadia. Spectators frequently hooted at black players, threw peanuts and bananas, and chanted various racial taunts and slogans.

While this was happening Garth Crooks was breaking into the Stoke City team after making an introduction to football in time-honoured fashion by kicking a football relentlessly up against a wall near where he lived. The repetitive noise was to prove too much for one particular couple who took exception to Crooks' passion for the sport. However, that very same couple were to prove life-long friends to Crooks and his family.

Crooks has gone on to view the game from all angles. Having played the game at the highest level for Stoke City, Tottenham Hotspur and Charlton Athletic and held a pivotal position with the Professional Footballers' Association (PFA), he is now making an impression in the media.

However, it was the relationship he and his family fostered in their adopted home of Stoke that not only set him up for professional football but helped him learn about an English culture that was alien to him and his parents.

Growing up in Stoke

"When I was around about seven years of age there was a square where I used to play football. I would play football on my own all day kicking this ball against the wall and basically practising.

"Then after a while this incessant knocking on the wall irritated some people. One of these was Pamela McKenzie. She introduced me to her husband, Eric McKenzie, and I got to know their family very well. Pamela and Eric introduced themselves to my mother and father and they became lifelong friends. It was interesting because they brought to me and my family an aspect of English culture that perhaps I would never had seen otherwise.

"They had friends called Harold and Jean Kirkham who would arrange parties for me and my sisters, take me away on occasions to help give my mother a bit of respite from bringing up five kids. To this day, I keep in touch with them. My mother and father always ask about them, they insist that I keep in touch. I do and they are part of my 'family' and in a remarkable sort of way they really gave me an insight, not just into the English culture but the English psyche.

"The English are generally understated. West Indians are generally rather flash! The English tend to be rather – let me get the right word – they are 'reserved'. West Indians tend to be rather loud.

"It was a wonderful time for me, because I became the bridge between my family and the familes which became our friends and my football was pivotal to everything. I could make sense of it all. I could articulate what was going on. If my parents were having an argument I would say 'it is alright it is not a fight it is an argument!' I had to convey that.

"The McKenzies would look and be almost fearful, like they were wondering 'What is happening?' I would say 'no, everything is OK. They are having an argument. This is a heated debate!' Sure enough, they grew to understand how we work. That was a fantastic development for me and for them to understand that.

"They became second parents to me. Where my parents couldn't spend time making sure that my English was OK and my education was OK, they helped with that. They became a really integral part of the family. They were fantastic people and I owe a great debt of gratitude to them. Sadly two of the family have died but they are still very much a part of what I do."

Crooks went on to do extremely well in the world of professional football. But his early story underscores the fact that footballers need their home lives to be positive safe havens in order to display their ability on a match day.

"As I grew up in Stoke it was very much about being focused and I simply wanted to be a professional footballer. That is all I wanted to be. I just wanted to be a player. I was encouraged every week because my house in Buckley Street was adjacent to the Buckley Street stand at Stoke City's Victoria Ground so I could hear the crowd during matches, everything. I was enthused and I loved the sound of the roar of the crowd. You could tell when the home team had scored and I knew when the away team had scored. I knew what the score was by listening to the crowd.

Growing up in Stoke

"My mother's sister's husband, Uncle Bernie, he loved his football and introduced me to the game but he was very West Indian in his outlook and he didn't like the English game. He thought it was dull although he thought the greatest player on the face of the earth was Rodney Marsh.

"I loved football but I had to work at it in my own mind. What style of football would I need to adopt to make me successful? So, over the years I worked that out. I desperately wanted to be a skilful player, I didn't want to be a functional player. Why? Because I wanted my community to think that I was a good player. That was important to me.

"I wanted to prove myself within my own community first and the wider community second.

"My mother and father were my inspiration. My mother and father are part of that community and I wanted them to be proud of their son. I wanted them to like what they saw. I wanted to personify the sort of sportsman that they recognised and all their sportsmen had razzmatazz, flair, exuberance; people like Muhammad Ali.

"Sometimes we had sportsmen who spent a little bit too much time on the glamour side of things but it was important to me. I didn't want my parents to think that I wasn't a good player. So again it was trying to marry two cultures. Saying that, at the time it was difficult for me to understand and articulate it. It was around about 14-15 or maybe 16-17 I started to do that."

Crooks' marvellous career saw him play with and against some of the greatest names the game has produced. Ossie Ardiles and Glenn Hoddle are just two of the stellar players Crooks worked with. He will always be remembered as the man who scored Spurs' equalizer prior to Ricky Villa's memorable winner when the North London side beat Manchester City in the FA Cup replay of 1981 at Wembley.

But before those heady days in the blue and white half of north London, Crooks' career and life was shaped by the ultimate England icon.

While he did not play with England's legendary 1966 World Cup winning goalkeeper Gordon Banks, Crooks had the misfortune, as he saw it at the time, to get advice from a man considered by many to be the greatest shot stopper of all time.

Banks was ruthless with young Crooks at Stoke but now that he is more mature, the former Spurs man knows the massive role Banks played in his development.

"Gordon saw my ability from the start but he thought I was very lazy. Yes, he was right and I have told him that so often.

"I have a huge regard for Gordon Banks. He was the best goalkeeper in the world, probably the best goalkeeper I have ever seen or worked with because I have worked with three of the best goalkeepers probably there have been. I have worked with Shilton, Clemence and Banks, closely with all three of them.

"I have beaten all three of them at some stage. I would say in order of ability; Banks, Shilton and then Clemence. Gary Lineker disagrees with me but that would be my three in that order. Gordon's first challenge was to either make me or break me. He came very close to breaking me.

"He just didn't let me off the hook. He wanted everything I did to be the best I could do. If it was folding towels, he wanted it to be meticulous. He wanted me to be in on time and, if possible, early. To be ready for work, ready to do whatever he wanted to do and at that time I was very cavalier in my approach."

Since their earliest appearance on the football scene, black footballers have had to deal with heavy stereotyping as well as opponents. Crooks was determined not to underpin the thoughts of a nation. Jokes circulate in the black community about so-called 'Caribbean time' where even with important things to do, life is sometimes taken at a leisurely pace. Crooks concurs.

"I think what it is; not sufficient importance is placed on certain things and if you are creating a structure then certain things have to be in place. Two things that have to be in place are discipline and application. Gordon made it his business to try and instil that in me, although it was whatever it took as far as he was concerned.

"I am grateful now, but at the time it was bloody hard. It was really, really hard because he was a tough taskmaster. He was a sergeant major. I can hear him shouting my name at the bottom of the dressing room and I would tremble and ask 'what have I done now?'

"He would run his finger across the dressing room wall and say 'There is dust here.' He would often say 'I have made it too easy for you.' The game is not that easy. That was his message. For two years he gave me hell."

Banks' harsh discipline on an impressionable youngster came on top of growing up in an area which had different values to those practised in the traditional West Indian family home. Even though

Stoke was considered home, it was not always the most agreeable place to be with a black skin, according to the articulate Crooks.

"I make no apologies in saying that the fact was that Stoke-on-Trent was a place which at the time was not welcoming. It was frightening. It was a small-minded town, Stoke-on-Trent; a city made up of five towns, and they were mining towns. The pottery business was its main source of income in those days and we are talking 1960s, 1970s. It was a tough town and I think they had a distrust, to be fair, a distrust of strangers and you had to prove your worth. You weren't there to loaf is how locals saw it. You weren't here to feed off the hard workers, if you like. Ironically the same sort of arguments still take place today all over the country. And I think we did our share of work. I certainly got great kudos, however, from being a footballer playing in a local town."

But even though he was eventually to become something of a local hero, Crooks had to stand up and fight on occasion. It was an attitude that remains with him today even though there are different opponents.

He recalls vividly one particular incident from his youth:

"It wouldn't have been the first time that I had to fight my way out of a corner. They were tough kids. I had to find my way out of a few situations. I remember leaving the club one day as an 18-year-old driving home and there were police in an unmarked car with their flashing lights. These coppers came over to me and said 'you black bastard, pull over!'"

His football status was the only thing that saved

him from a potentially dangerous situation. Luckily one of the officers in the car must have been a Stoke fan and said: "I know who he is, leave it."

"So it was a double-edged sword. I suppose you have got to roll with it. I am not saying that it was right but I learnt to roll with it. The good and the bad."

Crooks joined his hometown club as a sixteen-year-old in 1974. He went on to score fifty-three goals in one hundred and sixty-two appearances before joining Tottenham for £650,000. Leaving Stoke for the bright lights of London in 1980 was a dream come true.

He had survived the Potteries and unpleasant racist chanting at big grounds such as Anfield, St James' Park and Stamford Bridge to make a move to North London. It was to prove to be a perfect union. Of the abuse in the late 1970s he admitted: "In a strange sort of way while they were taking the piss out of me I was doing the business, so I was getting some personal satisfaction."

Doing the 'business' led to his transfer to Spurs and he was then on the launching pad to great things. Spurs as a club suffered its own prejudice. It was supposed to attract Jewish fans and thus its supporters and players were known as 'Yids'.

"I always wanted to be in London. Big club. I was honoured to be called a 'Yid' as opposed to a 'nigger' because it was almost like a term of endearment compared to what they could call me! There was a culture attached to Spurs and in some ways it was similar to the West Indian culture. I love the Jewish humour. I really did enjoy my time at Spurs and everything that came with it. It was a big club and we wanted to win things but first of all the club wanted to win things that was the thing. They wanted to succeed.

"I loved Stoke City football club because it taught me how to play football, but Tottenham taught me how to win things."

He certainly did manage to win medals, getting his hands on two FA Cup winners' medals, a League Cup winners' medal and a UEFA Cup winners' medal. He was also capped for England at Under-21 level. Crooks marked that international debut with a hat-trick to underpin his sense of occasion. After a short spell with Manchester United he spent two years with West Bromwich Albion before injury wrecked his career and he retired in 1990.

He was to become the first black chairman of the PFA in 1988, the 100th Anniversary of the Football League and an exciting time from a football politics point of view. It was a position that allowed his constant desire to talk about the development and progression of fellow black players. Indeed Crooks was one of the first players to stand up and speak out with regard to racism in football.

Crooks has always been an activist. In 1985 he founded the Sickle Cell Anaemia Research (SCAR) organisation which promoted awareness of the illness and raised funds for medical research and for support of sufferers. He has been involved in various forms of community work such as liaising with the Metropolitan Police, serving on the Notting Hill Carnival Committee and working with London Boys' Clubs to promote community values through football.

In short, Crooks has done as much as anyone to rid footballers of their negative stereotypes. Crooks opened the media door to players such as Ian Wright, Mark Bright and Robbie Earle, as the desire to engage former players on numerous panels has grown at pace.

Becoming chair of the powerful players' union was

ultimately to prove to be good practice for his media career.

"I was very aware of what I could and what I couldn't say. I sometimes say things now which would have been political suicide then. I have made some of my feelings known to the Football Association for example; I would never had done it then. It wouldn't have been tolerated.

"I wanted to be as successful as I possibly could and all the time forcing the game to recognise the contribution of black footballers. I am articulating that now. I wanted to be on those sort of terms then but I wanted the game to recognise the contribution.

"How could anybody celebrate my performance at Tottenham and then criticise Vince Hilaire in a manner that would be considered racist? He is a 'black bastard' but he is your hero. What kind of bollocks is that?

"So it was that rationale that I thought was unsustainable. Anybody with the slightest sense would think 'Hang on a second, how can you abuse one player and then celebrate Garth Crooks in my team the next?' That is nonsense. But people have started to address those issues."

Crooks' time as PFA chair was a tricky one. His tenure took in the disasters at Bradford, Heysel and Hillsborough but his relationship with Gordon Taylor, which remains as strong as ever, was key. Of Taylor, Crooks says:

"He is seen as a man who doesn't recognise colour. I think it is a rare quality and when you come across it, my God, is it special. I have worked with this man for over twenty years. We came through the Heysel disaster together, the Bradford disaster together and Hillsborough together… difficult times. We came through the identity card scheme together. We came through all of those and in all of those issues I saw a man who was at the very top of his trade.

"He had great administrative skills, great neg-otiating skills and he was everything that I wanted to be in terms of a top football administrator. The players were very lucky to have him and in 1990 when the Football League tried to snatch him I remember having a rather uncomfortable discussion with him and his wife. I told him 'You are not joining that lot' and of course he is still at the PFA."

Crooks' first role model is his mother. His whole outlook on life, like so many of his generation, is built on those precious family values that appear to have taken a back seat these days when the world's top footballers earn large sums of money and enjoy the kudos – and vices – that go with it.

"Whatever I have done, I have always been conscious of not letting down my mother. Anything, anything, but that. I have worked ever so hard all my life not to disappoint my family because they always expect better of me.

"I am a big man now but my father is always expecting better of me. They have got tremendous pleasure out of the success of their son simply because they can walk tall, that's all. If they can walk tall, I think that is all they have ever wanted.

"Making sure that I didn't bring any shame on my family and being accepted into the black community was always important to me. I just wonder today where that philosophy has gone. It was there once and it has disappeared and I don't know why that is. That is how I see it."

Crooks was a 1970s/80s pioneer who helped put black footballers on the map. But while he played his part, he is happy to place the plaudits on more gifted players who helped to illuminate the English game. And one particular name continues to be pushed to the front.

"Laurie Cunningham was without doubt the most naturally gifted black player that I have ever played with. John Barnes was a naturally gifted player, too, but I never played with him. To do what he did at Liverpool, bearing in mind that he was with great players and he is considered maybe one of the greatest, if you look at that Liverpool team they all looked to him as being an outstanding player."

Crooks, whose game was based on pace, intelligence and an eye for goal, has words of praise not just for the men that create and score goals – the hard currency of football – but also for the men who do the donkey work and consequently do not receive the same accolades as the front men. On reflection one defender in particular still makes the former Spurs man wince.

"I think Bob Hazel was a terrific competitor. He broke the mould. He would crack you in two as much as look at you. Who else is there? Defenders that I admired. One of the defenders that I liked was Chris Hughton. Chris I thought was fantastic. A Rolls Royce of a player, never went to ground, always stood on his feet. He could run you. He would have a battle with you. Whatever it took! He was consistent. He goes about his job at Spurs, with the same enthusiasm and the same focus as he did from day one, but you would never know that he was there. He is one of the more delightful, one of the most honest, one of the most wonderful guys I have ever had the pleasure to meet.

"Those two are the defenders to which I would give top marks. As for the forwards, I thought Luther Blissett was a tremendous trier. Great record. A bit mad. I wondered if he was mad because what's the point of sticking your head in there? Go for the next one was my view.

"Big Cyrille Regis was the [Didier] Drogba of his day. I would have paid £40million for him if I was a manager."

As the so-called black explosion gathered pace in the 1980s it was obvious that a camaraderie was developing among black players who were now becoming very much part of the fabric of the English game. One particular PFA awards evening made it clear to Crooks that the Black Pack were making an impression on football's social circuit as much as they were on the field of play.

"I remember Ray Wilkins commenting on our togetherness. We would congregate and get together because we used to have a great hoot. About a dozen black players all sitting there talking and having a great laugh in the hall at the Hilton. We were the loudest group. All the white players would be looking at us, wanting to be involved but they didn't know what was so funny. I remember Ray Wilkins saying 'how come every time we go to a game or event all the black boys are together?' I said 'Ray it's too hard to explain.'"

The easy answer was that black people like to party in the company of each other. There was a time when house parties, or 'blues', were a regular occurrence for members of the black community in England. They would normally take place on a Saturday night and consist of music, dancing, Caribbean cuisine, but most importantly a chance to catch up with friends. The bonding by black players at the Football Awards was just extension of that Caribbean revelry at a time when most of them were still not accepted by all of society, fans and teammates. It was one of the few occasions when players who were being racially abused every time they laced their boots could strike back and let the indigenous population know that they were here to stay.

Those fortunate enough to be playing now owe so much to those that paved the way.

Crooks continues:

"I would say it was intimidating because we could look after ourselves in all aspects. There was a lot of respect there. In those days the two Fashanu brothers were there. They were awesome. No-one messed with Justin or John because they could hurt people. Funny enough, though, on the field they were animals, off the field they were gentlemen. Also in the group were Hazell, Regis and Brendon Batson.

"We felt we had arrived. This wasn't an apology. We were here because we had a right to be here. We could play. Our white colleagues knew we could play and they would laugh and joke but when we got together it was very difficult for

white people to access that culture because we would return to who we were and what we knew.

"Occasionally we would break into patois [Caribbean dialect] and we would have fun and it was really, really good. You would get some guys like Vinnie Jones who was as comfortable in that environment as he was in his own, and that is why Vinnie became a real star with us.

"There were one or two others who had that ability as well. I suppose in this day and age, the pop culture being what it is, David Beckham is as popular in our community as Sol Campbell. Probably more so! Sol's a bit dull in comparison, love him as I do. You speak to black girls and they will talk about David Beckham so that is how things have changed."

Crooks' role with the PFA, and latterly as one of the most recognised faces of the BBC's football coverage, has kept him in touch with the game even though he is no longer scoring goals. He is forthright, but, as the negative stereotypes of black players in particular and sportsmen in general have shifted, maybe more importantly he is able to put his point of view across with a succinct alacrity that makes people take notice.

He is as ambitious in the media world as he was when he was playing. As ever, he has a story to tell about his early interest in the media.

"In 1981 during our Cup run, I became very aware of the media. I had never had such attention – and I loved it. I thought 'this is the future, this is where it's at. The proliferation of television and radio is where it is going to be.'

"The media train was ready to leave the station so

I had to quickly get on that train."

Having got his chance at Capital Radio, Crooks has gone on to work with some of the legendary names of TV and radio including the late, great Bobby Moore, Jonathan Pearce, Paul Dempsey, Sid Burke, Robbie Vincent and John Motson.

"I love it, it's flourishing and it is doing very well but it can end tomorrow. I think we are all one booking from being sent off. Look at Ron Atkinson, it can happen to anybody. I would hate to think that I would use profane statements like that because it is not part of my everyday language but the point I am making is that I think we are working in an environment where things can be so difficult. I have had a fantastic time. No complaints and if things changed I would probably become an agent."

While Crooks would be happy to represent players from all backgrounds his real concern centres on young black players who want to break into the game and see a career in playing football.

Wider society has no compunction in condemning some young black men as a menace to society. Crooks is of the opinion that sport, and especially football, can play a positive role for youngsters who feel that they have no place to go in life.

"I have a real concern about our black men. I think our black boys get a bad deal, yes, without a shadow of doubt. Where was I going to go if I didn't play football? What was I going to do? I'll tell you what I was going to do. I would have gone to youth training college but what would I have been there? Some sort of inner-city school doing what and going where? What would have been my ambitions? To be a PE teacher?

"Is it any wonder in this country that our black boys get so frustrated and pissed off that they go off the rails?"

Crooks, while contributing to and recognizing the progress that the sport has made in terms of race relations, is not convinced that the game presently reflects the diverse cultures in the United Kingdom. The make-up of the Football Association, responsible for running the national game, is indicative of Crooks' concerns.

"The Football Association are the national governing body. They control the sport in this country and the mechanisms and the structures that they put in place when they were formed in 1863 are still the mechanisms and structures today. The FA does not reflect football in the 21st century and the way it should be run and its structure."

While dismayed at some of the archaic thinking emanating from the people who run the game, Crooks anticipates continued progress by black footballers.

At one stage during the 2002 World Cup quarter-final against Brazil in Shizuoka there were, after substitutions, more black players than white wearing England shirts. They were Sol Campbell, Rio Ferdinand, Ashley Cole, Trevor Sinclair, Kieron Dyer, Darius Vassell and Emile Heskey.

The development of the African-Caribbean player was further underpinned during England's 2005 close season tour to the United States of America. The national side beat their hosts 2-1 in Chicago and their line-up included David James, Glen Johnson, Sol Campbell, Wes Brown, Ashley Cole, Jermaine Jenas and Kieran Richardson who made a double scoring debut in a lively match.

Among the substitutes who came on were Zat Knight (replacing Campbell) and Jermain Defoe (replacing Ashley Cole).

"Black players have added something very special to the English game, which was not there prior to their arrival. Call it what you want. A certain flair and exuberance. It has added some real spice to what was rather a dull dish.

"I think the black player bends himself to wanting to bring something to the game that makes, I think, his own community smile first.

"I mean Shaun Wright-Phillips is a lovely, quiet fellow and when I watch him play I feel very comfortable. He plays for the black player.

"One of the disappointments to me, when I saw Paul Ince, who made a fantastic contribution to the game, but the player who left West Ham didn't have the same skill and ability when he went to Old Trafford. He became another Bryan Robson.

"I would have loved him to become the best Paul Ince he could have been. Great contribution to the game but I think he had more skill than Bryan Robson. But what happened to it?

"I just hope we don't lose that side. Now obviously Arsène Wenger brings in black players. He brought over Thierry Henry not to be a John Radford; he brought him in to be Thierry Henry – and what a wonderful player he is. Those players Wenger brings in. Look at Lauren; stylish, lovely player, athletic strong. Kolo Toure; athletic, strong. Ashley Cole; box to box, top player. You look at those players and you feel they are black players and you are proud."

Crooks' praise is not just reserved for Arsenal, noted for their stylish play allied to athleticism. He pays tribute to Chelsea, who under the unique leadership of Jose Mourinho won the Premiership and Carling Cup in his first season in 2005 and repeated it in 2006.

With the likes of Claude Makelele, Didier Drogba and William Gallas in their side, the Blues from Stamford Bridge dominated both seasons. Crooks remembers a time when black players were not so welcome at the club from the King's Road.

Chelsea supporters were notorious for taunting black players, and not just those who played for the opposition. Paul Canoville, an elegant winger with a thunderous shot, was often the victim of racial abuse in the 1980s. How times have changed.

Crooks adds:

"What I find fascinating about this whole debate is the very people who are now talking about 'they [black players] are wonderful players I don't care what colour they are as long as they wear the shirt,' they were there first time around when I was playing and I am pleased they have changed their attitude because that is what it is about."

Chapter 9

The rise of John Barnes

WHEN BLACK PLAYERS represented the English national team in the 1980s they still had to endure racism from a section of England supporters. John Barnes was singled out for similar treatment both at home and abroad. In the summer of 1984 during the national team's tour of South America, he was subjected to booing and racial taunts by English fans.

These so-called 'fans' were clearly identifiable by the Union flags they displayed, which often had far-right slogans painted on them. Foreign black players were just as vulnerable, as was clearly demonstrated by the taunts aimed at Ruud Gullit in a friendly match at Wembley against Holland in 1988, while the Cameroon national side were also subjected to bigoted chanting during their visit in 1991.

Born in Kingston, Jamaica, Barnes will forever be known for his pace, general link play and eye for goal. He is arguably the most celebrated black England player to date having achieved so much at Watford and Liverpool and gained seventy-nine England caps in a truly illustrious career.

But when one looks just below the surface of Barnes' career, there were traumatic times for the son of a Jamaican army colonel. His early days at Liverpool were blighted as supporters questioned whether he wanted to play for the club. But even when he had established himself he was to become a big name target for the racists who followed both Liverpool's football clubs.

Who could ever forget the image of Barnes back-heeling a banana thrown by a so-called supporter during an Everton v. Liverpool match at Goodison Park in the late 1980s? It was a sign of dark times for black players. The situation seems light-years away now but Barnes and the rest had to be great survivors as well as players.

"I remember as far back as 1981 playing at places like Millwall and West Ham when you'd get the usual monkey noises and bananas being thrown onto the pitch," recalls Barnes, a player who still has question marks raised about his career. I believe it is fair to say that if Barnes had been white he would have been celebrated in much the same way as Gascoigne, Shearer and Lineker.

That trio were among the most celebrated players to pull on an England shirt. Gascoigne's mercurial play and tears made him, for a while, a national hero. Both Shearer and Lineker will forever be remembered for their goal-scoring efforts for England. But none of them gained as many caps for their country as Barnes, yet the former Liverpool man will always be considered a failure in an England shirt.

Surely winning 79 caps, under different managers, must mean that the man had what it takes. Stuart Pearce, not blessed with dazzling technical ability, has almost as many caps as Barnes yet he was fêted for his hardwork, honesty and love for a tackle. Barnes, with an eye for goal, ability to assist, and captivating left foot never gained the same sort of love. Without question he was never the same influential player at international level as he was at Liverpool, but the colour of his skin clearly did not help.

"It [racism] was almost an accepted part of society, so not very much was made of it. I considered them to be ignorant, so I never responded to it because I thought they would have won if it had affected my game."

Barnes' eloquence has resulted in him landing several jobs in the media, Ffrst as a pundit, more recently as a presenter of his own show and latterly as an interviewer.

Some of Barnes' football woe revolved around his inconsistent performances for the national side. His displays for England will always be severely questioned by those who wrongly thought he was not committed. Do those same critics remember the torrid abuse he took from his own supporters, most notably against San Marino at Wembley in February 1993?

Even before then his critics had poured scorn on his international efforts. Barnes had his own doubts regarding football but in this case his reticence had everything to do with the bitterly cold weather that greeted him and his family on 26 January 1976 when he first set foot in England.

"The thing I remember most was the bad weather. It was probably the coldest winter ever and it went on to be the hottest summer in 1976, but that particular winter was cold. I remember we were just about to land at Heathrow, and Chelsea's training ground was right by Heathrow and there were lots of football pitches.

"It was a Sunday morning, we landed about ten or eleven o'clock. I remember looking out of the window and all I saw was dozens of football matches going on as we came in to land. The thing that struck me most was that all of the kids playing had on the same kit so they were like proper teams. I played football in Jamaica but you would just put on any old shirt.

"As soon as I saw that I thought 'I am going to be playing for one of these teams.' I knew I was home. I had never been to England before, never seen snow and I thought it was cold before I had even landed, so I didn't know what it felt like playing on it but I could see football taking place and as soon as I saw that I was determined to be playing with one of those teams."

Barnes attended St Marylebone Grammar School in central London. He admits his school work took a beating because of football, all his energies being pushed into thinking about a career in the sport. It was to pay off handsomely in the end.

Like so many black youngsters in the 1970s Barnes was pushed towards a life of discipline and maintaining a good attitude by his family. He freely admits that while some of his friends were more skilful footballers than him, the discipline instilled by his parents gave him a solid platform, not just for football but for life.

"The discipline side of things always came from my dad because of his life in the army; life is all about discipline was his thinking".

Barnes may have been one of the most flamboyant players but while others from his community were content to just showboat and thrill, Barnes knew that hard work was the key to success.

"The perception of me when I started playing was being a disciplined and sometimes a boring left winger, started out when I first came to England. I played for a team called Stowes Boys club on the Harrow Road. I knew about good attitude and discipline.

"The team was made up of all black players. All of us wanted to score goals. We were all skilful and I was always an attacker. But really I was an attacking midfield player but when I went there I had to play centre back because no-one else wanted to! So I played centre back for four years because I was the most responsible one.

"We would always win by scores like 10-0. Everybody wanted to score hat-tricks and stuff like that but I played at the back. I suppose my dad always instilled in me the importance of a team ethic. Of course, when I went to Watford, and being a seventeen-year-old first year in a professional game, Graham Taylor obviously didn't want me to feel any pressure or too much responsibility so therefore I played left side midfield, left wing and he would say 'just go out and express yourself and enjoy yourself.' That was great!

"People know me as a player who liked to express himself but in terms of how I was actually brought up I was a very disciplined player.

"I suppose it really came round full circle when I was at Liverpool and I couldn't play on the wing any more. Then I went to play centre midfield. I just sat in front of the back four and once again just played a very disciplined role. People thought that a bit strange especially from what they remembered of me. But it wasn't difficult for me to do that at all."

Barnes cites his football-mad father and Germany's 1974 World Cup squad as his earliest football influences, while Wolfgang Overath was his favourite player.

Having dealt with the challenge of bitterly cold weather and getting used to snow for the first time, Barnes joined Watford. His father liked the disciplined regime that Graham Taylor ran at the Hertfordshire club so it was like a home from home for a player who, even at that age, had a cultured left foot.

It can only have helped Barnes' settling down period to be greeted by Luther Blissett who ensured that there was someone at the club to whom the impressionable Barnes could relate.

> "Luther was a great role model for me because Luther got on with everyone."

Barnes recalls having to get used to not only playing in the bitter cold, but dealing with a rather strange dialect. Thank goodness football is a universal language.

> "I had never met anyone from up north before and the accent was really strange. I had only been in England for four and a half years so I found it difficult. I even found it difficult just speaking to people from London. All of a sudden there were different accents and different attitudes.
>
> "Luther was the most popular player in the team, so that helped me because I was just seventeen years old. Getting into the first team and being the only black man in the team would take some doing, bearing in mind the amount of stick he was going to take. Some of it was tongue in cheek, some of it was like just messing around, but how do you know that?
>
> "Really, the way Luther responded to a lot of the banter was exemplary. Luther, for me, was the

best person to deal with it. If there was a twenty-six-year-old Ian Wright dealing with that banter it would have been completely different! But Luther was calmness personified, he was respected.

"In fact, indirectly, he had a big say in the way my career went because Luther got sent off, probably somebody called him a black bastard, I should imagine, against Newcastle the second game of the season.

"Obviously he got some racial abuse and I think he punched somebody. Because he was suspended I played the next match. Graham Taylor put me in the squad. I was on the bench for the first game, came on against Oldham for fifteen minutes and did really well. So the next game against Chelsea at Stamford Bridge, fourth game into the season, I did really, really well again. So then the manager said 'Right you stay in the team.'

"Then Luther came back because Luther had to be in the team but then somebody else dropped out and I played. So if Luther had not got sent off there was no way I would have played. That was my first full game in professional football. I was not even an apprentice or had even played in the youth team, I played one reserve game before I got in the first team. I would have been in the reserves maybe for two years maybe for one year, you don't know, without Luther's sending off. Luther was a great role model and he also helped me!"

Barnes was now on his way to the big time. His dazzling wing play was eye-catching. But so was the colour of his skin. Not surprisingly one of his first encounters with racism in football took place at West Ham United's then notorious Upton Park.

"I didn't really understand what they were saying anyway. Bobby Barnes was playing for them and it always struck me as odd that they were cheering Bobby and at the same time they were giving me all this abuse which led me to question what exactly racism was.

"It never affected me at all as a person. The way I see myself is that nobody can do anything to me that will make me have less self esteem, so therefore if the whole crowd shouted 'nigger' at me it is not going to make me feel bad.

"I considered those people to be ignorant so why would I show them the respect even to entertain whatever they were saying to me? It was like water off a duck's back."

These experiences while wearing the yellow shirt of Watford stood him in good stead in his early days at Anfield. Newspaper speculation suggested that the Watford wonder really wanted to move to Arsenal and saw Liverpool as, at best, second on his wish list once a transfer was in the offing. The newspaper headlines made life difficult for Barnes after he signed for the Merseyside club in 1987.

"When I first went to Liverpool there was a lot of negativity because there was a story about me snubbing Liverpool for Arsenal because Liverpool wanted to sign me in the January and I wanted to wait until the end of the season.

"God rest his soul, Emlyn Hughes wrote a little story about how dare he snub Liverpool and he was very critical when I first arrived. But after the first game of the season when I played really well at Bayern Munich, opinion changed slightly.

"Then, fortunately, the first three games were

away because they had a problem at the Kop end so we couldn't play at home. In those games we beat Arsenal, ironically. I must have scored two or three goals away from home so by the time it came to playing at Anfield the fans loved me."

Among Barnes' numerous anecdotes is this particular gem:

"There were two Liverpool supporters who went to Anfield. They got there at the same time every match – when you are walking to your seat you see the same people every match. You don't know who they are or where they live and they talk to you like they are your friends. Then when your team scores you celebrate together. So you have a little community of football fans and for the rest of the week you don't even know them.

"These two guys sat in the same seats every week and my friend used to sit in front of them. He said they would talk about me before the game, saying 'We don't want that coon coming here and Barnes this and Barnes that!'

"After I'd scored a goal at Anfield they soon stopped the whole coon thing and said 'We don't want him coming here.' Then, later, one of them looked at the other and said: 'You know that Barnes he is not as black as I thought.'

"This goes to show that if you score goals it doesn't really matter. Fortunately, because I did the business, I was OK. But that is why, as much as Liverpool fans say they love me, they actually love the number 10 shirt. Playing well for Liverpool is what it is all about.

"I know that had I failed I would have got more stick than if a white player had failed. As much as they love me as a black man who does well, they wouldn't love me as a black man that failed. I thought about it before I played for Liverpool. Even when I knew I was going there I thought 'I know if I don't play well it's going to be difficult.' But from the first game the way that everything just gelled with the team, and Peter Beardsley in particular, and the way everything went, I knew there was no way that it was not going to work."

Things fell into place so well that Liverpool, under player-manager Kenny Dalglish, won the title in swashbuckling style. Barnes, along with Peter Beardsley, Ray Houghton and John Aldridge moved the goal-posts as to how the game was played. Pace, movement and technical ability was to the forefront.

No wonder that Liverpool remain uppermost in football fans' minds, no matter which team they support. They set a template for great football teams. The fact that Barnes was so pivotal to that great, all-conquering side surely put black players in an increasingly better light.

Even though the mighty Reds possessed a great starting XI it was generally accepted that Barnes was the glue that held the first team together. The winger scored fifteen times in thirty-eight games as Liverpool equalled the then record of twenty-nine League games unbeaten from the start of the season and reached the FA Cup final, losing to Wimbledon. The impact of Barnes in that 1987-88 season earned him the respect of those who commentated on the game. He became the first black player to win the Football Writers' Footballer of the Year Award, winning it in 1988 and 1990. He also won the PFA Player of the Year Award in 1988.

His excellent form saw him collect an FA Cup final

winners' medal the following season, 22 goals and his second championship winners' medal.

Barnes' standing at the club was duly confirmed when Graeme Souness took over the management reins from Dalglish. Souness immediately made Barnes captain, a far cry from the days when his allegiance to the club was being questioned by sceptical fans.

Apart from handing Barnes the ultimate responsibility of leading a club of such great tradition, Souness switched the man who had made his name as a winger into a central midfield role. It worked like a dream. While his pace might have diminished due to injuries, his speed of thought had not and Barnes was now able to play his conductor's role from the very best position.

Roy Evans replaced Souness after the Scot's ultimately disappointing spell in charge and under the new manager, Barnes won a League Cup winners' medal in 1995. Two years later he joined Newcastle United, and a year later his services to the sport saw him receive an MBE.

A loan spell at Charlton Athletic was his last playing action before his much-chronicled and brief spell in charge of Glasgow Celtic made all the wrong headlines in 2000.

While his playing career at Anfield was recognised as a hit what patently did not work was Barnes' England career. Other great players such as Paul Gascoigne (57 caps) and Glenn Hoddle (53 caps) did not gain as many international caps as Barnes but he, for whatever reason, never seemed truly comfortable in an England shirt with the media and general public indifferent to his international performances. Although Hoddle struggled to win universal approval among England fans he was not treated like Barnes.

To blame his colour would be too simple and churlish. Barnes under-performed for England essentially because they did not play in the same manner as his club side. However, being black and under-achieving meant that Barnes was to get more grief simply because there was so much expectancy.

Barnes was the seventh black player to gain full England honours on making his debut against Northern Ireland in 1983, His outstanding, magical moment for the national side came against Brazil in the world famous Maracana Stadium in 1984. Barnes single-handedly took on the South Americans' defence and went on to score as fine an individual goal as you could wish to see.

Sadly, Barnes did not have much time to reminisce over his wonder strike. Racists, calling themselves England fans, were inexplicably allowed on the England plane home from Brazil and they let it be known in no uncertain terms that great goal or not they would not easily accept a black man in an England shirt.

While his resolve and family values could help ward off such distractions it was still a puzzle to Barnes as to how the racist mob could be allowed to journey with the England side in the first place.

Barnes was frequently singled out for booing by England crowds. The question many observers posed was would he have taken the same flak had he been white? It was a totally ludicrous situation that an England player should be verbally pummelled by the team's own supporters and so blatantly.

"Obviously there are reasons behind everything, but it was something I have to accept – and it was also a question of timing. There were very few technical players around then, only the likes of Glenn Hoddle and Chris Waddle. England

114

didn't play that way. Supporters liked Peter Reid. They liked hard-working players who got stuck in, so therefore, while it was not a case of playing at the wrong time for England because you play at the time that you were meant to play in, players like Glenn and I, and others of that type, were always deemed to be inconsistent."

The game against the minnows of San Marino at Wembley in 1993 was the only occasion that the boo boys looked like winning. Barnes admits that he would have been happy to have been taken off but the resolve of Graham Taylor saw him stick it out.

"Things weren't helped when there was a piece in the *Daily Mirror* before the match that reckoned because I wasn't born in England I was not committed to the cause. So this whole thing was blown out of proportion the day before the San Marino game.

"I was not doing well but neither was anybody else. So, of course, they focused on me because I was not supposed to be true to the cause. They liked Terry Butcher and Stuart Pearce.

"Now, look just how far football has come. A friend of mine supports Arsenal, where he has a season ticket, and is as patriotic as you like. Before Arsène Wenger arrived at Highbury my friend was adamant that he was no longer going to watch the team he had supported for years. 'If Wenger comes I am not going.' Now, because of the success, he is there all the time!

"So, therefore, we are in a different era now but during my time it was like, 'Is he true to the cause because he is not English?'

"You have bad games, days when you have messed up and you want the ground to open and

115

swallow you up, but you still want to be on the field and you still want to play and you think 'I can do better.'

"I have to say that that game against San Marino was the only time I wanted to be taken off. When I had bad games I would think 'shit that was really embarrassing' but I wanted to stay on because I felt I could do something about it. But on the occasion against little San Marino I have to admit I wanted to come off.

"Maybe a different manager would have taken me off because he could see what was going on. The players were embarrassed. In fact the press were embarrassed afterwards because normally they would have given me stick for playing badly but they didn't give me any because they were too embarrassed about the blatant stick I took.

"Graham Taylor told me afterwards, 'I wouldn't let them win. No matter how bad you were playing I was not going to you take off. Whoever the best player was, he was coming off before you.'

"I am really glad he did that because Graham Taylor was a really clever man and a right thinking man and he said 'this is more important than a game of football.'

"But now if anything hurts me it is that people knew that racism was happening then but said nothing about it. Any journalist over forty would have known what was going on back then but they never said a word. Now all of a sudden after Emile Heskey got stick in Macedonia the same reporters became the big drivers of Kick Racism out of Football. They said after that match it was unacceptable and put it on the front pages. Why wasn't it on the front pages back when I was playing? All of a sudden everybody is jumping on this bandwagon of like 'isn't this terrible' and 'let's sack Ron Atkinson.'

"The way Liverpool played to the way that England played was different. In the England set-up I was stuck out on the left and they played in straight lines but at Liverpool I had much more freedom in not only what I did but in terms of the way the rest of the team played. We brought the ball out from the back with Alan Hansen and people who played in midfield. The midfield players would play two touch football. We also dominated possession.

"I remember while playing for England, the majority of times I played – I would say ninety per cent of the time, no matter who we played, whether it be Tunisia or Argentina – our opponents dominated possession and dominated the game. We would win because we had strong players and centre forwards scoring goals from set pieces, but in terms of the way the game went you would argue, take the goals aside, the opposition played as well if not better than us because of their technical ability. In England it was not about that. Therefore the technical players didn't shine. So I feel that was the main reason for my failure at international level, if you want to call it that."

It is a mystery to me that Barnes could be considered a failure. At club level he was the linchpin in a team full of star names. Peter Beardsley, John Aldridge and Ian Rush were all to benefit from his accurate, visionary play. His switch into central midfield helped him to showcase a versatility not previously demonstrated by a black player in English football.

Two league titles, one FA Cup and one League Cup

plus his England caps cannot be considered a shabby return but many feel that Barnes would have had even more respect if his England career had been smoother. Nevertheless he is more than happy with what he achieved.

"I enjoyed playing for the country I was picked to play for. I couldn't have enjoyed playing for Jamaica more than I played for England. When they ask 'did I enjoy playing for England?' I say I enjoyed playing for the team I was representing, which happened to be England. I have never been a believer that you have to be prouder to be English. At that time that was what it was all about. We were English so we were better; we should have more pride playing for England than other players have playing for their country."

After retiring Barnes was to link up again with his first manager at Anfield, Kenny Dalglish, when the Scot asked him to become manager at Celtic, where Dalglish was Director of Football.

Many questioned whether it was the right move for a relative novice but others saw it as a plum job for a black manager who had a huge profile. Many within Barnes' West Indian community could be heard saying a collective 'at last' to an appointment that had been a long time coming. In the end, however, Barnes' move into a tracksuit did not pave the way for other black managers. Indeed, it was such a short lived disaster that in fact many thought it was an indelible stain on the prospects of those who looked to follow Barnes' lead.

"I am sure the directors did not want me but Kenny said 'if I am coming then John's coming too!' So that in itself made it very difficult, because while Kenny was very supportive of me nobody else was and they really thought Kenny had made a mistake.

"I didn't know that at the start, not when I signed the contract. But within the first week of being there I quickly realised it. They expected Kenny to be more hands on and I was being questioned. But I thought it was not going to be a problem because I knew we could challenge Rangers. We won the first twelve matches, drew one and lost one, to Rangers, so we were five points behind them. I thought to myself it was going to be very difficult because even then I was still getting the questions. What more can you do?

"If you come second there it is just complete doom. But we were just five points behind Rangers. We drew with them just before the winter break at the end of December, I won Manager of the Month for December and I was sacked in January after we lost to Inverness Caledonian Thistle in the Cup.

"I had signed Ian Wright to score goals, to fill in until Henrik Larsson came back from injury. But of course Wrighty came up on good money and the other players were not on such good money, so there was jealousy. Some players were not earning half what Wrighty was earning, so we had those problems there as well. I didn't understand the reason for it. There was a lot of politics involved in that.

"Whatever else was going on I know I didn't encounter any racism. I encountered being English much more than racism because they don't like the English. That kind of helped me a little bit because I kept saying 'I am from Jamaica, I am not English.' So therefore I was not even interested in anything off the pitch or the training field."

Barnes was sacked after less than eight months. A string of poor results and that shock cup defeat by Inverness Caledonian Thistle, coupled with him allegedly losing the dressing room, resulted in him being shown the exit. Barnes turned what many would regard as an ordeal on its head, insisting it has sharpened his appetite for football management. He is keen to get back on the management merry-go-round.

It has been suggested that Barnes was sacked too early by Celtic and also that he had jumped in too deep in taking one of the biggest jobs in football for his first shot at management.

"I lost my job but it was not traumatic. The desire hasn't gone and my confidence has not gone. I have no doubts about myself. We were six points behind Rangers when I left, but, as I said, unfortunately that is deemed as failure in Scotland. We were already in the semi-final of a cup we eventually went on to win, while Rangers had been knocked out. Unfortunately, there were not enough people backing me or who believed in me, and my position was undermined."

Barnes points to the broken leg suffered by Swedish top scorer Henrik Larsson as the turning point of his reign in Glasgow.

Since being sacked, Barnes has turned to the media world which so many players see as a viable and lucrative alternative to coaching. He is the face of Channel Five's football coverage but still hankers after a managerial role.

"I don't think anybody could have played

under Graham Taylor and not be interested in management. He really encompasses what total football management is. I think Terry Venables encompasses what coaching is about but in terms of the psychology, whatever, Sam Allardyce is talking about now what Graham Taylor was doing back then.

"We had a psychologist, we went to hypno-therapists, and we had dieticians. So Graham Taylor made a big impression on me. You couldn't help being helped by playing under him, in terms of the tactics that go into football matches, the training methods, everything. It is something that I would definitely like to do again.

"If I could have gone straight back in I would have. I have not had the luxury of turning down job offers, but I do miss football management and I am very keen to get back into the game. I don't know how low I would go, but if a Second or Third Division club had ambition, prospects and the possibility of success, I would think of joining them."

Whether he gets the opportunity remains to be seen. The lack of black managers is still a major debate within the game. Barnes may well suffer by being negatively labelled after his debacle at Celtic Park.

"I try not to be disappointed about anything because everything happens the way it is supposed to happen. If I had control over it and it didn't happen then I would be disappointed, but I have no control over it so therefore I am not.

"I am optimistic things will change. I suppose you become less optimistic the more years go

121

on. I am hopeful it will happen sooner rather than later but it is hard. As time goes on you do become probably a little bit disillusioned. I would say more disillusioned than disappointed."

The word enigma has often been attached to Barnes. Even when he is not playing or managing he courts controversy. The latest furore took place in early 2005 and involved a Football Association DVD which featured the top England players of all time.

The media whipped up a storm by pointing out that it included no black players. To many observers, Barnes should have been included but, just like his England displays, there is room for argument.

"I didn't even want to be in it! That was such a ridiculous situation. That was political correctness gone mad. I wouldn't have chosen any other black players to be in either. I am not going to put myself in for a start. Should Paul Ince be in it? Is Rio better than Bobby Moore?

"If Pele had been English obviously he would have been in it, but I don't think there were any black players that were obviously in the top twenty England players. For the FA to then say 'OK, we are going to take it off the shelves and then we are going to redo it' was silly. So therefore there were only two black players included, so am I going to complain because there should be more. It is crazy!"

In my view the FA's DVD was not worth all the fuss. Football is a game of opinions that generally differ. However, to then include black players – to be seen to be politically correct – was the real howler by the FA. John Barnes, with 79 caps, should have been a contender at least. But bearing in mind some of the torrid abuse he received when he did represent England this would have smacked of hypocrisy. The likes of Des Walker, Sol Campbell and Paul Ince could have sneaked in but no doubt there would have been a large percentage of England fans who would have disagreed with their inclusion. While black footballers increasingly play a part in the England set up, one has yet to genuinely command respect in the same way as an Alan Shearer or John Terry.

For a man who still struggles to walk through Liverpool city centre without cars honking and people wanting to shake his hand or just say hello, Barnes is remarkably downbeat about what he has achieved in the game. He understands the adulation but does not go looking for it.

The history of black footballers in England will mark him down as the first true black superstar. Other players, for varying reasons, never properly fulfilled their potential. Barnes was the first to do so over a sustained period. He had the ability, played in a great club side which won honours and played seventy-nine senior international matches for his adopted country.

"I find it hard to accept the recognition because I think it is for other people to decide. What I did was to be very fortunate to have been playing and doing something that I loved and getting paid for it. That is as far as it goes for me.

"When the likes of Kieron Dyer and Jermaine Jenas say I was a role model for them they surprise me every time because I didn't play football to be appreciated. As much as people talk about playing football because they want to be appreciated and playing in a way that they want to be remembered I didn't do that. I did it for selfish reasons maybe. I did it because I loved doing it.

"That is why it never interested me in retiring at the top. The only reason I finished playing was because I got an offer to manage Celtic.

"If I hadn't managed Celtic I would have been happy to have gone on to play for a Third Division team. I think people who want to retire at the top do it not because they love football but because they want to be remembered as being one of the best players for their club.

"That is not how I want to be remembered. I didn't even want to be remembered. How important is it? OK it is nice, but are they going to pay my mortgage or get me a ticket to Liverpool? I can't even get into the ground now! How much are you really remembered? It is nice when that happens but how important is it for them to be talking about me? It is not important at all. It doesn't affect me."

Chapter 10

John Fashanu and the Crazy Gang

JOHN FASHANU ALSO suffered while wearing the Three Lions of England. While Barnes gained seventy-nine caps, Fashanu gained just two but his story is as intriguing as the former Liverpool man's.

John Fashanu is a man who knows a thing or two about abuse. The brother of the late Justin, who in 1981 became the first black player to cost £1million, has been at the receiving end as a player and, more recently, as an entrepreneur.

Fashanu, a gregarious and likeable character with the same non-stickability as the Teflon range of kitchenware, has always courted controversy, none more so than the match-fixing drama that was to take him to the brink and cost him the best part of £1million in court costs.

But just like his playing days, the player dubbed 'Fash the Bash' has more than just survived. He freely admits that he was no Laurie Cunningham or John Barnes but the attributes he did possess – athleticism, brawn and bravery – were put to good use during a career which saw him play for Norwich City, Crystal Palace, Lincoln City, Millwall, Wimbledon and Aston Villa.

Even in his formative years, Fashanu, one of the first African heritage players to make their mark in the modern era, had an eye on the rewards that playing football could bring.

"Football for me became important the day I received my first pay cheque because I wanted to use football as a way of empowerment," recalls the original footballer-turned-TV star (no matter what Ian Wright has to say!)

"In turn I could put a roof over the head of my mother and my father. I had a firm belief that I wanted to improve my mother's life, my father's life and also my sister's life from a young age, so that was really my real drive.

"It wasn't about wanting to score goals. It wasn't about wanting to play football. It was about wanting to bring home a nice pay cheque so that I could put food on the table for my mother and father and also my sister who needed help."

The story of the football-mad Fashanu brothers, sons of a Nigerian barrister, and born in Kensington, London, gained headlines because they were sent to a Barnado's home. Years later they were fostered by Alf and Betty Jackson and brought up in Attleborough in Norfolk, a far cry from their African roots.

But the younger of the two Fashanus maintains that his natural mother was the inspiration behind him and his brother's notable careers.

"Because I was fostered, my white mother and father didn't really encourage my career because they didn't understand the concept of playing football.

"They didn't understand how big it was or the passion we had. But my mother Pearl, my black mother, she understood what we wanted to do. She could see that we could actually put money on the table and it was a good thing for us because she was a single mother and I think we didn't get as much support as we would have liked, but she was still quite supportive."

Justin was the first to make a breakthrough into football when he played for the England Youth and Under-21 teams and made his professional debut at Norwich City in 1979. He scored BBC TV's *Match of the Day*'s goal of the season for Norwich against Liverpool in 1980 and all seemed set fair for a considerable career.

At the time he signed for Brian Clough's Nottingham Forest, Justin Fashanu was in a heterosexual relationship but he was soon drawn to Nottingham's gay scene. When Clough discovered this Fashanu was suspended. However, he still turned up for training, whereupon Clough had the police escort him off the premises.

After that, Fashanu's career, also hampered by a knee injury, was in free-fall. A number of clubs attempted to resurrect it but none managed to.

In May 1998 he was found hanged in a lock-up garage in Shoreditch in east London. The coroner for Poplar, Dr Stephen Ming Chan, recorded a verdict of suicide.

His younger brother, John, was not as gifted but as well as two England caps he won an FA Cup winners' medal with Wimbledon and respect in certain quarters for his self belief and tenacity.

That tenacity still marks his post-playing career. Having hung up his boots, John Fashanu has been determined to champion the cause of black footballers in general and African players in particular.

His football life got underway as an associate schoolboy with Cambridge United, and he was signed by Norwich in October 1979. He made his debut in 1981 as a substitute at home to Shrewsbury Town.

Goals, the hard currency by which all strikers are judged, were hard to come by and after a loan period with Crystal Palace he was transferred to Lincoln City for £15,000 in September 1983. This move lit the touchpaper.

A good scoring record at Sincil Bank (eleven in thirty-six games) captured the imagination of Millwall who signed him in November 1984. As Fashanu was scoring goals he was also building himself a fearful reputation. He was big, strong and quick, traits that were now becoming vital commodities in the English game.

Wimbledon signed him for £125,000 in March 1986 after fifty games for Milwall had seen him bag twelve goals. His style of play was pivotal to the rise and rise of the Dons in the late 1980s with promotion to Division One and that unexpected FA Cup final win over Liverpool.

In 276 league matches for Wimbledon, Fashanu scored 107 times. That rate of scoring was to ensure an England call up and as his star continued to rise he earned another lucrative move, this time to Aston Villa.

One can sense that having been something of a pioneer himself he is proud of what the current crop of black players are achieving.

"You know when I see Didier Drogba, Jay-Jay Okocha and some of the other boys who are coming through, like Lomano Lua Lua, I am proud that they have continued what we started.
"I am sure if you speak to the Cyrille Regises of this world and the Garth Crookes' as well they would be proud of what we did. It is a generation thing which has been handed on and I think that even with the money side of things, each generation you speak to was paid in that particular time good amounts of money, which is relevant."

Luther Blissett, Watford, AC Milan and England, has an Italian anarchist society named after him!

*John Barnes played 79 times for England and was one of the stars of the
all-conquering Liverpool team in the 1980s.*

Mark Walters won only one England cap but had a glittering career with Aston Villa, Rangers in Glasgow and Liverpool.

Paul Ince became the first black player to captain the England senior team when they played the USA in 1993.

Paul Elliott, a commanding central defender, experienced three footballing cultures, playing in England, Italy and Scotland.

Hope Powell was the first woman and black person to coach an England football team.

The effervescent Ian Wright made football acceptable to a whole new generation of black football fans.

Andrew Cole changed the attitude of Newcastle United fans towards black play-ers before going on to forge an all-black striking partnership with Dwight Yorke at Manchester United.

Sol Campbell, who made a short but eventful journey from Tottenham Hotspur to Arsenal, was the second black player to lead the senior England team.

Rio Ferdinand has become an essential part of the Manchester United and England team but has attracted headlines for other reasons.

Les Ferdinand, a cousin of Rio, preceded him in the England side.

Les Blues and Les Gunners. Thierry Henry, Patrick Vieira and William Gallas before the 2006 World Cup final, although Vieira was at Juventus and Gallas at Chelsea at the time.

Ruud Gullitt was the Premiership's first black and foreign manager, leading Chelsea to an FA Cup victory in 1997. He also managed Newcastle.

Jermain Defoe, unlucky not to play in the 2006 World Cup, was an instant hit under new England manager Steve McLaren.

Nigel Reo-Coker, captain of West Ham and one of the Premiership's greatest young players. He was on standby for the 2006 World Cup.

Theo Walcott attracted much negative publicity after the decision to take him, at 17, to the 2006 World Cup but seems certain to justify the fee that Arsenal paid Southampton – a downpayment of £5m which could reach £12m.

John Fashanu and the Crazy Gang

Fashanu is of the belief that black players have made their mark at home and abroad not just because of their technical ability.

The former Wimbledon front man has no hesitation in suggesting that physique gives black footballers a distinct edge over their white counterparts. Fashanu is adamant that England's failure to succeed in Euro 2000 was due largely to the fact that the national side did not have enough black players in the starting XI.

"I stand by that. I think that the world is realizing that the game of football is about being an athlete. You have to have athleticism. You have to be able to get from one eighteen yard box to the next – and that's a seventy yard sprint! Why do you think Patrick Vieira is regarded as one of the best players in the world? Because he can get there, he has got the engine to do it. Very rarely do you have to run one hundred yards in football.

"The maximum you have to really sprint is probably twenty-five yards but you have got to have people who can get there – backwards and forwards. And the black generation can do that. Black races are born for sport more so than white people.

"I used to know that if I was playing against white players I could always beat them at a standing jump. So I knew from a corner there was no point me running around everywhere trying to lose my marker because I knew physically and athletically I could jump higher.

"Players knew it and so did managers. Everyone in the game knew. It was an unspoken word. They knew that if you were playing against black players they were always faster than the white players. It was a foregone conclusion. I knew I could push the ball and then just go straight by them. Teddy Sheringham was one of the players who first acknowledged it and said that black players are faster and stronger than white players and that it was something we all have to live with.

"I think it has always been a taboo subject because I think it has almost offended white people or worried them in a certain way. I think it is also a case of black people not wanting to offend white people and also wanting to keep your position in the team. The less you say, the better it is.

"I can remember when Garth Crooks was playing. Garth Crooks was faster and quicker than everybody and was also a hell of a header of the ball. Cyrille Regis was awesome when he broke forward with his 20 yard sprints and dashes. We can all remember him when he was at West Bromwich and he would just power his way through the white boys.

"When I was playing against the likes of Paul Elliott I knew that was the day that I was going to have to work for my corn. I knew it was going to be a hell of a day. I knew I would get up in a bad mood thinking those boys were going to make me work hard. But I also knew when I was playing against Arsenal against Tony Adams, Steve Bould and Martin Keown that psychologically they would not enjoy it.

"Physically they weren't going to be able to challenge me. I knew that I was stronger. I knew that for all the battles that Martin Keown would give me that I was tougher than him because mentally I was tougher because I was a black man.

John Fashanu and the Crazy Gang

"A famous England coach told me 'Get it up Crooksy because he doesn't like it' – but that was absolute nonsense as he actually played better when he was up against tough tackling defenders. Yes, nobody likes to be kicked up the rear forty times in a match but at the end of the day you deal with it.

"They said things like black players didn't like the cold; well there are a lot of black players who don't like the cold sure but there are a lot of white players who don't like the heat!

"Why don't we reverse that and say 'OK, when it's hot here they don't like it and they can't play.' Any minority is going to be persecuted. From the blacks to the Jews and unfortunately we as black players were persecuted."

Fashanu had another sort of opponent to face in 1995 when *The Sun* newspaper made match-fixing allegations against him, Hans Segers and Bruce Grobelaar. They were arrested but eventually found not guilty – although they had to pay their own legal expenses, which for Fashanu was a hefty £650,000.

Having survived this bad press, Fashanu landed a role as presenter of the popular all-action TV show *Gladiators*, which pitted contestants against super-fit gladiators in trials of strength, speed and stamina.

Today football fans marvel at the pace and power of Thierry Henry and Rio Ferdinand. While appreciating what those two modern icons have brought to the game, Fashanu is quick to point out that several of his football generation were doing the same long before.

"We were doing it for twenty years in the previous period. People didn't appreciate the pace I had until it became so bloody obvious that I could

just knock the ball ahead of me, give somebody
three yards and still catch them!

"Thierry is doing it now but you've now got 35
cameras around the football pitch and everybody
is appreciating the play and we can all see
it. Thierry is like a gazelle but there was many
players before him who were like that. Tony Sealy
was one. If you can tell me of a black player who
is slow I'll give you a million pounds!"

What Fashanu is not so certain about is whether
one day an all-black XI will ever be able to represent
the senior England team. There has been much
debate on the taboo subject. And if the growing black
representation in the Premiership is anything to go by
it has to be a distinct possibility.

All the signs point to the fact that that dream could
be reality. During England's summer tour of the United
States in 2005 there were, at one time or another, some
seven black players wearing the famous Three Lions
proudly on their chest. But Fash does not believe that
the powers-that-be would be comfortable with that
scenario.

"Anybody who says that they will be able to see
that day is either dreaming or a damn liar because
that will never happen. That is like saying let's go
to Russia and see whether you have got people
from Afghanistan who will be dominant in the
Russian team. It's impossible. At the end of the
day, yes, the black man is born and becomes
English but at the end of the day it is the English
who invented the game of football and, of course,
it is their sport.

"However, even if we were born here and our
ancestors were born here we are obviously

descendents from Africa. So as black people we can never say that we are English one hundred per cent. It is silly for us to think like that. I always say 'don't go to Russia and try and make as much money as the Russians. Don't go to China and try and live as well as the Chinese because although this is our country it is also not our country.

"It is our country when we are all good boys, but it is not our country if it kicks off and there are some problems, as I think that history has shown, especially in a lot of my cases!

"When I was going through the match fixing case, the world's most publicised case, I was then the Nigerian-born John Fashanu. But when I was winning the FA Cup – having played for England and played in Europe for Aston Villa against Inter Milan – I was the wonderful, proud, English born John Fashanu.

"It is the foreign players, black players included, who revolutionised the game of English football. They are the ones who stopped the boys going out drinking. Chelsea's John Terry has a weight problem and he will always have a weight problem. He is the first to admit that. That is not said in a rude way because he is a fantastic player. But because now he has got so many foreign players around him do you think John Terry will be going out to a pub and drinking and eating fish and chips?

"The culture has changed. Now he is eating pasta and eggs with the yolk taken out. Players now have pure Evian water flown in especially from the Swiss Alps. People understand the changes but it is the foreign players who brought these changes."

It is also foreign coaches who have been responsible for a culture change in the English game. Arsène Wenger's arrival at Arsenal was one of the most significant reasons why footballers, of all colours, changed their way of thinking. The fact that Arsenal's eye-catching success has been achieved with so many black players has been a catalyst for clubs at home and abroad. Wenger has developed many a player but his two outstanding success have been Patrick Vieira and Thierry Henry, who were not succeeding in Italy. Wenger added dietary and technical savvy to the athletic technique of the two superstars. He was also able to do that with a generation of players who had not before considered this approach. The careers of Tony Adams, Nigel Winterburn, Lee Dixon, Steve Bould and Martin Keown were all extended by the man dubbed 'The Professor'.

England had a foreign coach in Sven Goran Eriksson who had no issue with picking black players for his squad or starting XI. Fashanu, however, is of the opinion that there are still numerous hang ups surrounding the make-up of the England national side.

Never one to duck an issue, Fashanu states:

"I can only speak for myself but I know that when I was playing for England I was by far the best player in the country at the time because I knew I had to be twice as good as any other white player to get in. Even to be seen.

"I got in the team the year before, after I had scored twenty-three goals in the league, and that was two goals less than Alan Smith who was the leading goal scorer. And I was playing for a little club called Wimbledon. So I was by far the best player, strength-wise, speed-wise and in goal scoring ability and I still wasn't getting called up."

Up to and including the 2006 World Cup, there have been fifty-three black players who have proudly pulled on the England senior shirt. Anderson got the ball rolling in November 1978 with Theo Walcott, controversially selected for the tournament even though he had never played in the Premiership and Eriksson had never seen him play, being the fifty-third. Representing England, however, has been a traumatic experience for some of them and Fashanu was no different.

To be booed by the opposition is part and parcel of football. It is almost a sign of respect. But to be booed by your own fans as Fashanu was against Scotland at Hampden Park in May 1989 was a numbing experience to say the least.

> "The abuse I got playing for England was unprecedented. Playing for England was not a happy experience for me. Seeing John Barnes being booed and hearing the monkey chants going on and bananas; no, it was not a nice experience.
> "I always talk about the saddest time of my life which was coming out of the tunnel against England v. Chile with everyone booing me. My own supporters booing me!
> "It was a just a mockery of why you put on the white shirt. At least when I was booed during my time at Wimbledon the whole team was booed, but to be singled out because of the colour of your skin is totally outrageous.
> "The average black player does not get abused now unless he does something radically wrong but most people realise that abuse is wrong. That's

not to say they don't do it. But most people in football stadiums realise calling someone a 'black so-and-so' or a 'nigger' wrong and they could be pulled up on it.

"Before, there was no awareness, no exposure at all and a lot of the kids did it because they thought it was like peer pressure, like smoking. If you smoked, everyone was going to smoke. But now at least people realise the obscenities are wrong. We have got a long way to go but everybody is certainly raising the awareness of racism in football."

In January 1995, Manchester United star Eric Cantona shocked not just the football world when he took his own stance against racism by delivering a kung-fu style drop-kick at a Crystal Palace fan who abused him at Selhurst Park. Cantona responded to a stream of racist abuse from Crystal 'fan' Matthew Simmons by jumping over a barrier and assaulting him. Already one of the most newsworthy of players, this attack put Cantona on front and back pages for weeks on end.

His actions caused a stir within the football fraternity. However, many black footballers were chuckling to themselves. The Frenchman was sen-tenced to two weeks in prison, reduced to one hundred and twenty hours community service. He was fined the maximum his contract allowed by Manchester United and another £10,000 by an FA disciplinary commission, who also banned him from the game for nine months. Many a black player wondered what would have happened had one of them had perpetrated such a crime, no matter what the provocation. The consensus was that they might never have played again.

Fashanu sees it this way:

"I understood Cantona's feelings. I sympathised with him and I was one who wanted to give him a pat him on the back because I could never have got away with it. But being Eric Cantona and playing for mighty Manchester United, the biggest club in the world, he had a hell of a lot more chance of getting away with it than John Fashanu playing for one of the smallest clubs and being black.

"There were times when I wanted to react. I remember when I was playing at Goodison Park. That game was a hotbed of racism and I remember during the match one voice all the time saying 'You nigger, you black sambo, you wog, coon.' It seemed to go on for three days.

"Towards the end of the match I thought to myself 'I've had enough of this.' I went into the crowd and looked at the boy and he must have been about 16 or 17. I had Denis Wise and Vinnie Jones around me and they said: 'Where are you going Fash?' I said 'I've got to sort this out!'

"I walked into the stand, grabbed hold of the boy, held on to him and said 'citizen's arrest!' I'd had enough. The boy was in shock and horror and he tried to pull away but I had him in a sort of martial arts grip so he couldn't move.

"The more he actually pulled away the more he hurt himself. It was starting to kick off because everybody was going 'what the hell is happening here?'

"In all fairness, the police came and arrested him. They questioned him and asked me later if I wanted him to be charged. Wisey and the Jones boy came into the stand with me to give me backup, as did a few of the other lads, and that was my first stand against racism."

The togetherness Fashanu and his teammates displayed was indicative of the Wimbledon spirit in the 1980s. Dubbed 'The Crazy Gang' because of their extreme behaviour towards each other and opponents, the unfashionable south London club were to become perennial party-poopers.

In 1988 they defied massive odds to beat the aristocrats of Liverpool in the FA Cup Final. It will forever be regarded as one of football's seismic shocks.

The famed Wimbledon spirit, according to Fashanu, was born out of black street culture.

"Oh yes, we definitely took the culture off the black man – an urban street culture. The music system in the dressing room always had R&B or soul music pumping out of it. Heaven forbid anybody who put some white music in there!

"They would have had the crap beaten out of them. At one stage we had nine black players at Wimbledon. It was just a fantastic atmosphere. Eric Young, Laurie Cunningham and of course Jonesy – who is blacker than me! When we went out to a nightclub all together Jonesy was the first on the dance floor dancing with all the black lads. Absolutely fantastic."

Jones was one of those white players who was always comfortable in the company of black players. Since retiring Jones has turned to acting and taken Hollywood by storm with notable performances in hit movies such as *Lock, Stock & Two Smoking Barrels* He has retained his close friendship with Fashanu even though acting assignments mean that he is generally on location.

John Fashanu and the Crazy Gang

"Great times, great era, great camaraderie and I think because there were so many black lads all the lads got together and became a family. We had a very strong bond between us. There was Terry Phelan, Roger Joseph, Eric Young, Robbie Earle, myself, Mitchell Thomas, Carlton Fairweather and Andy Clarke. It was crazy how many black players were in there. Absolutely crazy, but fantastic."

Fashanu believes that his Wimbledon, of which he was spiritual leader, established a template for today's Premiership performers. There is now a 'cool' culture in the English top flight and that includes how goals are celebrated by the black football fraternity.

"The culture of the Premiership is as the culture of the film world, as the culture of the music industry. It is black. The world now picks up its vibe from black America.

"Even the Presidents of the United States from Clinton to Bush have been seen doing high fives. That is a black sign of endearment. The different languages that black people speak, when we shake hands or click our fingers, the different moves, the bling bling in the ears and around the neck come from the P Diddys and the black world generally.

"The cap not sitting straight on your head. You have got white boys out there now trying to be black. You have got white boys out there who think they are black. You have got white boys out there who will literally talk to you and say 'hey man, what's up man.' You think 'well'!!

"As for the goal celebrations, Wrighty, Thierry, they are the people who express themselves.

At Wimbledon we were doing our dances and everything else. These are all black moves because we were all black people expressing ourselves.

"The white boys have picked up on it. The back flips, they were done by the black lads who were coming over here. They are all athletes and it is great to see the white boys are now doing the same thing but there are not so many white boys who are athletic enough to be able to do those flips to be quite truthful. We were spontaneous."

The progress of black players does not surprise Fashanu. Of his own heroes, Fashanu says:

"Cyrille Regis was always everyone's hero because of the explosive way he played football. My late brother Justin was a hero of mine because of the magnificent goals he scored. Laurie Cunningham was one of the top idols that I had ever seen. To me he epitomised soul, rhythm, music and everything good with football.

"The strides black players have made has been like a fine wine, they have got better with age. It doesn't surprise me. Every day more and more black footballers in this country are being respected and appreciated more and more. It just doesn't stop.

"I mean the Chelsea scene is great. Have you seen how many black players they have? It's a great advertisement for black players around the world. The Premiership was won in 2005 and 2006 by a team that was nearly seventy per cent black. It was a massive achievement and the team that came second in 2005 was a team that was nearly ninety per cent black and that was Arsenal. I mean all these things make a great story. The players have a story to tell and I think managers are realizing, and have woken up to the fact that black players are so valuable in so many ways.

"If managers are after a striker they now say 'We want a black striker. We want a 6ft speedy striker, make him black. We want a defender, tall, strong, aggressive, make him black.'

"The emergence of black footballers will always help communities all over the world because it gives us someone to relate to. It gives us somebody to idolise. It gives us somebody we can believe in. If he can do it, we can do it, is the thinking because we all appreciate that the boy who is the idol today, yesterday was working in a factory with me.

"Sixty per cent of black players come from broken families, so we all know where we are going. For the first time in this generation we have role models for our youth and our young people to believe in.

"The next step is to have role models in the business world because black people are not only successful in sport and music, there are so many other industries where there is ability. Sport and music are the only two industries where we cannot be held down."

The 1980s saw a considerable increase in the number of black players. Indeed, a number of players such as Arsenal's Ian Wright were first spotted playing non-league football.

By the end of the decade, clubs with no black players on their books were very much in a minority. Although overt racism inside football clubs was beginning to decline, on the terraces it remained a problem. Also, black supporters continued to be a rarity at stadia across the country, even in areas where there were substantial local black populations. These two negative aspects were, during the 1970s and for much of the 1980s, consistently overlooked by football clubs, the game's authorities and also by the British government.

But by the late 1980s, a number of high profile clubs with little previous history of signing black players made significant moves into the transfer market in this direction.

At Liverpool, John Barnes was signed for a fee of nearly £1million from Watford, while at Leeds United, Rod and Ray Wallace were captured from Southampton. Viv Anderson and Paul Ince moved from London's Arsenal and West Ham respectively, to Manchester United, while Mark Walters left Aston Villa to join Glasgow Rangers, a team idoliszd by a largely Protestant following, and with a hooligan element espousing Loyalist and far-right causes. The Glasgow club banned some season ticket holders following racist abuse aimed at Walters.

Chapter 11

A different kind of bigotry

WHEN MARK WALTERS was breaking new ground by becoming the first black player to join Rangers, across the city at Celtic Park, and an opponent in the 'Old Firm' games, was his boyhood friend and former Aston Villa teammate Paul Elliott who had signed for Celtic.

Elliott joined the club in July 1989 from Pisa, having left Aston Villa two years before. If there were racist issues to be dealt with by a black player in Italy, there was racism and bigotry of a different sort in Scottish football culture.

> "I thought I went from the frying pan to the fire when I left England to go to Italy; God knows I went from the fire into a volcano I think in Scotland," was how Elliott remembers his time in the green and white of Celtic.
>
> "Scotland is an amazing country because, I suppose, I inherited bigotry that was one hundred years old. When I had players in the dressing room telling me that their families didn't get on because they had different names, I was thinking, 'well I can just about understand black and white but I don't understand white clashing with white and all the name-calling and the bigotry issue that exist between them.'

"I went from one thing into another and I always said to people that the reason why I enjoyed Old Firm games so much was because all the attention was diverted to Mo Johnston!"

Johnston had signed for Rangers and while he was not the first Catholic to be signed by them, as is sometimes thought – Rangers already had John Spencer on their books – he was an ex-Celtic player and hugely controversial as such.

Elliott recalls:

"I was out of the front line. The bizarre thing is that the Scots are a wonderful race. The Scottish, the Irish, the blacks; we have all suffered that level of social exclusion, that deprivation. And that is why you will find that those three races generally get on well. If you go to a pub in Kilburn or you go to a place in Scotland there is a sort of synergy there. It has come from decades of relatable problems.

"Obviously we all know that in a perfect world you should treat people how you want to be treated yourself and get respect by being a decent human being but it doesn't work like that. I think your standing within the game could be used to good effect. But you have got to deliver on the pitch first and luckily in both Italy and Scotland it was a question of going there and imposing myself against the odds and then using that platform to do positive things.

"I wasn't too shocked or surprised at the racism when I went to Celtic because I had experienced it throughout my career in England and in Italy."

He was so successful with Pisa that he was named best foreign defender in Serie A. Elliott doubled up by winning the Scottish Player of the Year in 1991 to confirm that a black Englishman abroad could rise above the racism and cultural issues of playing in a foreign land and still deliver where it matters most: on the field of play.

Walters began his career with Aston Villa before moving north to join Rangers, where he won three Premier League championship medals and two Scottish League Cup medals.

A £1.2million transfer saw him join Liverpool in 1991 where he won an FA Cup winners' medal. Injury problems with John Barnes gave Walters his chance at Anfield but he was never quite capable of filling Barnes' boots. He never quite hit the heights expected of him and his days were numbered as Liverpool's 'Spice Boys' emerged in the shape of Steve McManaman and Robbie Fowler. On leaving Merseyside, Walters had stints at Southampton and Swindon Town before joining Bristol Rovers on a free transfer in 1999. He now works with Aston Villa's academy.

Elliott and Walters first met in their teens, when both represented England at schoolboy level. They were to become teammates at Aston Villa before fate meant that they opposed each other in football's most heated derby.

While football rivalry meant they had to put their friendship on hold for ninety minutes whenever the Old Firm clashed, they both did much to break down the cultural barriers that existed in a city that had a very clear view not only on football but more important issues such as religion and colour.

"We were two mates playing for the two biggest clubs in Scotland, and we made an impact as players, educating peoples' minds and hopefully we were judged as players and not on the colour of our skins."

145

The judgements made on Elliott and Walters' time in Glasgow, Elliott believes, means that black players can now move north of the Border and not face the hostility they did.

"It is no big deal now. It is just what I call the fixtures and fittings of the modern day game. They look at a player and say, 'Can he do us a job? Is he good enough?' Colour is not an issue now. Because, ultimately, I think the way, since the Bosman ruling and the wider implications of that, everybody wants success it doesn't matter where you come from. It is about what you have, what can you deliver. The prerequisite now is if clubs believe you have something to offer them."

Elliott could be described as a glutton for punishment, moving to the racist football hotbeds of Italy and Scotland, but he capped that when he left Glasgow for Chelsea's Stamford Bridge at a time when the Blues certainly provided a threat to players of colour. Chelsea's fans had a notorious history of abusing their own black footballers, odd since players such as Paul Canoville, Frank Sinclair and Eddie Newton served the club so well in less glamorous times than those being witnessed by the King's Road club's supporters nowadays.

Elliott is as eloquent and elegant in front of a microphone as he was during his playing career. Recalling that he says:

"When I was in Italy in 1987 it was an extremely difficult time. In all honesty it was more rewarding when I went back to Chelsea in '91 because I sensed that attitudes were better, it was more progressive. The major catalyst was the Kick It Out campaign, which I've been involved with for many years.

A different kind of bigotry

"Firstly in Italy, there were cultural issues, environmental issues and, I soon realised, having looked at previous British players who had gone there, the most important thing for me was to learn the language. At least then I never felt excluded. I could attempt to understand what was going on around me. That was my first priority and to be fair it worked out well. I was speaking the language fluently after six months. I always say that I went a boy and came back a man.

"I was only twenty-three when I went there. I was very young and having been thrust into that environment it was extremely difficult to come to terms with it. I have no doubt about that, having played at some of the venues and experienced the racism.

"In all fairness, it never surprised me bearing in mind I had come from England. Racism at football grounds particularly in the north of England was still prevalent so I suppose going to Italy made me realise it was not just a domestic issue. It was an issue all over Europe."

"The experience stood me in good stead. At that point I represented the second generation of black players trying to make their way in the game."

But while doing that he was, he admits, often the subject of monkey-chanting and racist booing every time he touched the ball, in particular in one match against Roma.

"My family had travelled over to watch me as well and they were disturbed. I think that was probably one of the worse occasions because I must have been the only black player on the field.

"Racism was constantly there. You could feel it. You knew when the ball went out of play. That was difficult. I must say that was tough.

"I looked at my parents and how hard they have fought and struggled back in the sixties, the social exclusion, and the difficulty they had. I just took that and saw the resolve and how it shaped them for years to come. And you take that resolve with you, don't you? I think if I look at myself it was that sort of psychological strength, a mindset that helped. That vigour my family showed in their hard times, that mental capacity; it sort of follows me in my life and in my work now."

Being the only black player at Pisa meant that Elliott's only daily allies were his teammates. "I think they were embarrassed because they were thinking 'There is a problem here.' These were the people that you went out with. You socialised with them and they were thinking 'How can people behave in such a derogatory and disrespectful fashion?'

"I think they were embarrassed but I think what gave them confidence was to see the way that I handled it. I never used the racism issue as an excuse to affect my performance. If anything I used it as motivation. The same way I did in England previously. I just said 'hey I am going to go out there and show you how good I am and impose myself and my characteristics on the game.' Because ultimately I think that is the best way. If they can see it is affecting you, and your body language suggests it is, then no doubt they will come at you with even more vigour. So it was just about application."

During his two seasons at Pisa, Elliott, who mixed

considerable technique with strength and pace, was to face some of the biggest names in football.

AC Milan had Franco Baresi, Marco Van Basten, Ruud Gullit and Frank Rijkaard as their mainstays while a certain Diego Maradona was pulling the strings for Napoli. It was all part of a wonderful football education for Elliott.

"I couldn't ignore the financial aspect either. I recognised that I was a young man and I saw life like a journey. I suppose from a professional point of view Italy was, arguably even then, the finest league in the world and being wanted by a club that was prepared to invest in me told me that professionally I was facing a wonderful challenge.

"When I recall my debut against AC Milan I remember looking at their team sheet and not recognising a lot of the names who were going to be star names in the future.

"I tell you what, I found out ninety odd minutes later! My second game was against a certain gentleman called Mr Maradona so when you realise the magnitude of that you think 'Hey, this is colossal.'

"I think I felt it was hard to settle initially because I was put in this world where there was massive media intensity. The fact that I was a foreign player and as then each club was allowed only two foreigners there was a massive level of expectation. And the intensity in that world from a journalistic point of view was immense. These people want to know everything about you. I suppose, being the type of guy that I am, I said 'well let's attack this with real vigour. Give it my best shot. Go and enjoy yourself and make your family proud and make the most of the opportunity there.' It was one hell of an experience."

It is no surprise then that Elliott is now to be regularly seen providing expert analysis on Serie A games for Eurosport. To listen to him talk about his experience on foreign fields is to listen to a man who, despite the grief, could draw so many positives out of his time in Italy.

"I have kept many friends in Italy. I do a lot of business in Italy. I have learnt a language and I obviously work for Eurosport and so I think there have been immense benefits. But I think at that point, certainly from a professional point of view, it was just a wonderful experience. Yes, there were issues there. There was racism there and the shame is that it is still prevalent today.

"When you look at a lot of what has gone on, Italy is still a beautiful country. Classy people, classy race, but the reality is, in the same sentence, there are serious issues there. If you look at English clubs which have played in Europe, if you look at international matches, we cannot disguise the fact, so it is about how committed are the authorities to nullifying that?"

Elliott's career was ended after a tackle from Liverpool's Dean Saunders at Anfield. Elliott sued the Liverpool striker, claiming the challenge was reckless and that Saunders had dived in with his feet up.

After lengthy proceedings, the judge accepted that although Saunders did go in with his feet up, the seemingly offensive posture was in fact a defensive measure in the heat of the moment to avoid injury himself. Thus Saunders' actions were not in breach of his duty of care to Elliott.

A different kind of bigotry

The end, at just twenty-eight, meant Elliott had to find another way to put bread on the table.

Elliott's career at Chelsea was cut short when he was forced to retire. The technically accomplished defender should have been a genuine candidate for coaching or management but he never felt comfortable enough to make that step.

> "There were offers within the first four or five years after I came out of the game but it never felt right. It never felt fulfilling. Even now people say to me 'But Paul, you have played in England, you have been to Scotland, you have been to Italy, you are doing this and that in the media; isn't there an opportunity for all that in terms of management?'.
>
> "But I said to myself I don't really feel that it would be fulfilling. I already feel I am serving and influencing and in a way I wouldn't have the same level of satisfaction. And anyway the only guarantee in management is that you are going to get the sack! I think I understand the game and I understand people and I can work with people. But going into management or coaching just wasn't right."

Some former players have, rightly or wrongly, chosen to moan and complain about being denied an opportunity within their sport but Elliott decided to counter attack and remain upbeat about what the future holds for black players past and present. He is now an accomplished broadcaster, although the bulk of his time and considerable energy is spent campaigning against racism as a special advisor alongside Garth Crooks to the Commission for Racial Equality and running a football academy.

"I think there is a depth now of good people in this current generation who are sort of in their prime and while the game has been very good to that generation financially, the reality is all money does is buy you time. You still have to wake up with the motivation because you can't live in a nightclub 24/7, or in the bar or whatever.

"However, you still have to have a purpose. I would like to think now that there is a depth to this current generation from say twenty-five to thirty-two where there is a lot of talent to whom I would encourage to get into the coaching. A lot of them want to get into it now and that is where the recruitment procedures are important. But what they have to do is get themselves qualified first and foremost".

Many of those struggling to get management/coaching opportunities would beg to differ, having gained the qualifications and still not been shown the courtesy given to some of their peers.

Chris Ramsey, formerly coach to the England Under-20 team, is an example of how the football merry-go-round would appear to be designed so that if a black coach falls off he stays off. Ramsey, now Assistant Academy Manager/Head of Player Development at Premiership Tottenham Hotspur, failed to get any opportunity after being ousted from his coaching post at Luton Town in 2000. Ramsey, who played in the FA Cup final for Brighton & Hove Albion against Manchester United in 1983, had to move to the United States before he was offered a route back in to the English game when the London club came calling.

Yet managers, with fewer qualifications can fall off the aforementioned merry-go-round and get back on within no time at all.

A different kind of bigotry

Elliott says, "Like in any job, football has its ups and downs. Football is a world and a law unto itself. I just think the fact is that this generation have got to get themselves qualified, get their badges, and work within the game like any other business. If you want to become a reporter what do you do? You get yourself qualified, you network with people. It is easier in football because it is this strange little island with everybody on it.

> "That is the way I look at it. You have got to go in there and get connected. You work with good people and you know there are people that have all that and still have not got through the door. That is a fact. But that is one of the areas that we have recognised now.

"I don't like to harp on about the past but there are still issues. There is still a lot of work to be done. But equally, give respect to the progress that has been made today."

Among Elliott's aims for the Commission for Racial Equality is an evaluation of equal opportunities policies, a review of the recruitment and selection policy and its application to managers, administrators, coaches, trainers, scouts and players within football.

> "I want to serve. I am a businessman. I am a husband with a wife and family and you have got to protect your corner first. But what else can you do with your life after that? I just realise that it is important for me, despite football being good to me, and it is just my way of just trying to serve and affect people because I know there is still so much work to be done.
>
> "Football is a wonderful sport regardless of race, creed, colour or gender. There are tremendous

people now taking responsibility to deal with this problem and the ignorant minority. I'm very optimistic about the medium and long-term future.

"Everybody has a choice, whether they want to be in the front line or the back line. I just feel that with my knowledge, my experience and capacity to deliver it and penetrate people's minds it is important for me to make a positive contribution.

"A lot of people out there in prominent positions choose to do nothing. That is their choice. Everybody has a choice.

"Do you walk away? Or do you say you 'No, what I want to do is challenge?' I want to affect things but in a very constructive and positive way and at times I have to be radical. I accept that as well. So, what you have to realise though, if everybody was disillusioned and walked away what would you be left with? Would there be evolvement? Would there be the progress that has been made if twenty years ago everybody had turned their backs? What would be happening now? Would there be twenty-five per cent of the ethnic minorities playing in the game at the moment? There wouldn't be.

"There are still other issues. We all know about the lack of representation on the terraces or in the boardrooms or the administration or the coaching sector and also the lack of representation in the Asian community. I am fully aware of that. I see it as a 4x100 relay race. Somebody has run one hundred metres before they hand the baton to somebody else who has to take it on to the next level."

Chapter 12

Kick It Out

OVERT RACISM ON the terraces of football grounds began to decline in the late 1980s, perhaps as a result of the high profile transfer of black players but also because of the success of local black players at Arsenal. That served to attract more black fans to Arsenal matches and to counter racism (at least on the surface) among local fans.

At Liverpool, the signings of John Barnes, Mark Walters, Michael Thomas, David James and Phil Babb led not only to a reduction in overt racism among the club's fans, but encouraged a small number of black and Asian supporters to the club's home games.

At Leeds United, where the problem of racism had long been a feature of a vocal minority of home support, the signings of black players and the launch of an anti-racist campaign involving supporters, the local Trades Council, the police and Leeds players, went some way towards curbing racist chanting and far-right activities in and around the Elland Road stadium (see Leeds TUC & AFA, 1987).

However, a highly publicised incident involving an attack in January 2000 on a young Asian which implicated two of the club's players, Jonathan Woodgate and Lee Bowyer, arguably set back some of the progress being made in these areas.

In addition to these local campaigns, the cause of 'kicking racism out of football' was taken up on a national level, especially since the emergence of the post-Hillsborough period of reconstruction and modernization of the professional game in Britain.

New legislation, introduced in 1991, which outlawed racist chanting at football matches, gave the police new powers to arrest those fans who per-sisted in it. The work of a number of organisations, including the Football Supporters' Association, the Professional Footballers' Association, the Comm-ission for Racial Equality, the Football Trust and football fanzines contributed to challenging both hooligan and racist behaviour at football stadia.

In the early part of the new millennium top clubs in England were recruiting players from all over the globe – many of whom were black. On the one hand this 'new cosmopolitanism' might have further diminished overt racism among fans and club staff, but on the other it possibly closed off avenues for those British blacks and Asians who had ambitions to become professional footballers.

It is clear, too, that the acceptance of foreign players in England depends on their compliance with certain normative qualities of English football culture which assume that the game (and its players) is aggressive, tough and manly.

The rise and rise of the black footballer has been aided and abetted by the Kick It Out Organisation. The campaign – Let's Kick Racism Out of Football – was established in 1983. The organisation works throughout football and educational and community sectors to challenge racism and work for positive change. It is supported by the game's governing bodies including the PFA, the FA Premier League, the FA and the Football Foundation.

Internationally KIO plays a leading role in the Football Against Racism in Europe (FARE) network and has been cited as an example of good practice by the European governing body, UEFA, the world governing body, FIFA, the Council of Europe, the European Commission, European parliamentarians and the British Council.

Since its inception, the campaign has worked diligently with past and present players in an attempt to root out racism from football. While progress has been made there is still much to be done according to Piara Powar, its director.

"I think when the campaign was first set up there were still some very obvious problems. There was still racist chanting going on, there was still lots of abuse and football stadiums were still very much no go areas for black people other than players.

"It was easier to walk down the streets and easier to go to school and not expect to be abused. It was easier to just go about your everyday life, but football stadiums were the sort of isolated areas where I think it was still acceptable to indulge in whatever prejudices you had. Moving on from that I think what was needed was to educate people, to educate clubs, as to what they needed to do. People then began to understand that racial abuse, whether it was directed to the players or other fans, was not good for the game.

"We can't pretend that it is just the campaign's work that has made the difference. It went together with the gentrification of the sport. There is the fact that people can now be seen on CCTV cameras. If there are problems it is easier to pick them out and stewards are better trained and so forth. And as that got better, our agendas moved as well, more towards looking at complexities in the future."

Among the campaign's core priorities are working with the professional game by offering advice and guidance on all aspects of race equality. The campaign also seeks to address young people within schools, colleges and youth organisations. Other target audiences are catered for as KIO attempts to raise the issue of Asians becoming professional footballers and to build local ethnic minority communities to engage with professional clubs and the structures of the game.

The professional game, and the Premiership in particular, is the standard bearer for football, and the lack of representation of black people within it more than suggests that stereotypes have yet to be kicked into touch.

Research by Kick It Out has discovered that racism is endemic at the top level of the game. Blacks and ethnic minorities are massively under-represented and are not given the same opportunities as others.

A sport which uses black players when it suits, discards them quickly once they hang up their boots. Blacks and Asians represent just two per cent of those who wield control in football's richest league. Compare that figure to twenty-seven per cent of players being black and it can be seen that a genuine problem clearly exists.

While KIO has educated many within the game there is still so much to do according to its director.

"We have had some very bruising battles with some of the authorities. I am talking about the Football Association, I am talking about the leagues, I am talking about many of the clubs. Up until even, say, two years ago there were clubs inviting the likes of Bernard Manning into banqueting suites and gentlemen's nights and that kind of stuff. Those sorts of things still go on but I don't think you will see Bernard Manning, a comedian noted for his so-called jokes against the black community, appearing in many football places now.

"Educating the clubs has been a battle. To watch a Premiership match now, with black players playing integral roles, you would imagine that all has been well on the racism front for some time. That has not been the case.

"Clyde Best, during his days at West Ham, must have half expected abuse. But to think that players now are totally devoid of abuse at their place of work would be dangerous.

"We haven't really had cause to take people at, say, Arsenal or Manchester United to task but certainly in the past clubs like Chelsea, Leeds United, Sheffield Wednesday, when they were in the top flight, and Everton have had challenges. With a lot of these clubs it wasn't even about their fan base, it was more about what the management of the club was and wasn't doing. Often we would see abuse not being acted on. And you would have things going on in non-playing areas too.

"I say we haven't had any battles with the likes of Arsenal for obvious reasons because they have always been a lot more progressive but we have had, for example, a complaint. I remember it being reported in the London *Evening Standard* that there was a comic in one of those hospitality areas and he was making all sorts of racist jokes. Arsenal acted very quickly. I think the issue for us is that other clubs get very defensive."

When ITV pundit Ron Atkinson called Chelsea defender Marcel Desailly a 'f****** lazy thick nigger', not only the football world was in shock. Wider society was stunned that in the so-called modern era, a white man could still be heard describing a black man in the lowest terms possible.

The conclusion was that Atkinson, who, it has to be said, had been so instrumental in the career of so many black footballers, was at odds with society. His views, captured when he thought he was off-air, and his attitude were reported as those of a dinosaur.

But were they? Atkinson grew up at a time when it was thought to be OK to mix football's industrial language with a racist slant. What the incident did show was that Kick It Out's work in attempting to prevent black footballers being abused in the workplace is set for extra time.

The former Manchester United and Aston Villa manager has attracted attention in the past for his often clumsy on-air comments and eccentric turn-of-phrase.

He has provided summaries at five World Cups, six European Championships and many other major matches for ITV including Champions League and FA Cup finals. On being sacked from his ITV post and from providing analysis for the *Guardian*, he said he had made "a stupid mistake" - which he regretted - and pointed to his track record of bringing on black players during his coaching career, particularly at West Brom.

Atkinson had concentrated on being a pundit since leaving management in May 1999, when he failed to prevent Nottingham Forest's relegation from top flight football.

Should Atkinson be allowed back into football? Some would say rightly that even those that have killed or maimed get granted a pardon. While Atkinson's 'crime' pales into insignificance compared to those transgressions, he did undo most of the good work he had done in the past in relation to encouraging and developing black footballers. He should be forgiven but his comments will never be forgotten by those who heard them and, more importantly, by the black players who considered Atkinson was a manager they could trust.

It can take years to build a positive reputation but Atkinson has found that in the time it takes to score a goal, a mere second, a good name can be irrevocably tarnished. His name has been tainted and the punishment of losing his well-paid jobs was a small price to pay. He has popped up subsequently on our screens doing all manner of TV work. Rather than be remembered as the man that did so much for African-Caribbean footballers, he will be forever tainted with his TV gaffe.

England's infamous friendly international against Spain in November 2004 also showed that KIO is still much needed. England duo Shaun Wright-Phillips and Ashley Cole were the prime victims at the Santiago Bernabéu, home of Real Madrid, of abuse that embarrassed not only the Spanish nation but the watching football world.

The world governing body, FIFA, fined the Spanish Football Federation a paltry £44,750. That meagre punishment reflected exactly what sort of priority the game's rulers have given racism. The fact that they also took into account the racist abuse which surfaced the night before in the Under-21 equivalent between the two countries, shows that wanton disregard towards black players is not at the top of FIFA's agenda.

I believe the England players should have voted with their feet that night. The sight of the men who wear the Three Lions on their chest leaving the field of play in a high profile match, played out in front of a global audience, would have had much more weight than a decade's worth of Kick It Out's month of action, traditionally held in October to coincide with Black History Month. However, the Football Association's hierarchy (management, captain and Soho Square officials) decided to do nothing, stating that a withdrawal of the players was not on their agenda and probably would have caused even more problems and been a victory for the racists.

That last point is open to debate; a players' strike in effect would have been a short, sharp jolt not just to the perpetrators but to the rest of the global football fraternity. Without question, by staying on the field of play, England missed an opportunity to make a collective statement of intent. Well-meaning campaigns, well-meaning statements, T-shirts and badges alone will not stop those that abuse black players.

That said, Powar is of the opinion that in the United Kingdom at least progress has certainly been made.

"I think we have seen a lot of progress. Absolutely. We now have a basic acceptance, and it is very basic, but we have a basic acceptance from everybody that racism is wrong and that is on a very generic level. Moving on from there, we have a better understanding of what needs to be done. So we started off a long time ago with this ten point plan which was around before I was.

"We are now moving on to asking clubs to look at themselves and to ask questions about who they employ and how they employ them. Who is sitting in the stands and how they are getting out to people. We have had steward training programmes and so on and so forth.

"So I think we have seen a lot of progress. I think

almost so much so that when we now see the problems internationally, the England v, Spain game for example, a sense of righteousness is a little hard to take sometimes when you know that there are still other problems in England to be dealt with."

With more and more football clubs understanding the true value of black footballers, there might have been a school of thought that suggested that with safety in numbers, the players themselves would have been spared abuse because they were not in isolation in the same way that Arthur Wharton, Walter Tull and Clyde Best would have been.

However, this has not been the case. In fact the growth of black players seems to have infuriated the bigots even further.

On Saturday 28 September 2002, Arsenal fielded nine non-white players against Leeds at Elland Road. Arsenal manager Arsène Wenger fielded Ashley Cole, Sol Campbell, Kolo Toure, Lauren, Patrick Vieira, Gilberto Silva, Thierry Henry, Sylvain Wiltord, Nwankwo Kanu and, for good measure, Jermaine Pennant came on as a substitute. David Seaman and Pascal Cygan were the other two players.

The white rose club's supporters have never been overly tolerant of black players despite the fact that some of them idolised Albert Johanneson and the announcement and sight of the Arsenal side that day brought much negative comment in the crowd.

Once the visitors got into their glorious stride however, the mood changed to grudging admiration; such was the athleticism and pace of Arsenal's 4-1 victory.

Power adds:

"The numbers of black footballers grew in a way

that they were now deemed to be a threat. That's when the issues begin to get difficult. I think if you relate to people in a way that is in any way less than as a full human being then that will present problems. Whether you are doing it appreciatively or not.

"So, for example, I think that some of the comments that Arsène Wenger sometimes makes can be counter-productive. He talks about the athleticism and power and speed of this or that player and I think that those are the sort of attributes a lot of people associate with black players.

"It has been interesting recently because it is harder now for a British-born player to get into the game, because of the number of foreign players if you like, and because of the terms on which they can be bought in.

"So it is interesting now to see how those problems level out. We have seen a lot of black players now in the lower leagues, more than we have ever seen before, because people are just sort of saying 'OK, I want to play football, I will play at whatever level I can.'"

There was a time when black players were seen to be making up the numbers. That stereotype has moved on to be replaced by the realisation that black players are now at the forefront of the game being played at the highest level.

While players like Thierry Henry and Shaun Wright-Phillips make headlines when they are confronted by racism, the black players in the lower leagues just have to live with it and that is a situation that KIO is trying desperately to address.

"In football the top level makes all the headlines.

And if we can use the top level to send messages down to the grass roots that's all good. What we have found is that as the problem at the top has decreased so it has at the bottom. But having said that there is still quite a complicated picture.

"In the lower leagues we have got issues where three or four seasons ago during the last game of the season we had a banana thrown at a black player. You can't imagine that happening three seasons ago in the Premier League but lower down it happens. So from the top level we think that has led to changes but there are still issues at the grass roots. The grass roots being, I guess, Championship and below.

"At lower levels there are still old school managers. I remember Nathan Blake who challenged Bobby Gould over remarks he made, and now I think things like that have hopefully sent out a bit of a message to some of those old school managers as to the way they treat black players.

"Then, of course, there are the Ron Atkinsons of this world. It is going to be very difficult to challenge their thinking. But hopefully that generation is sort of phasing itself out of the game. I think some of them just take what we do for granted and are quite happy to.

"I think what you get there is a more localised vibe. If there has been a story in the local paper or the regional news about asylum seekers, or if an African player turns up, he is more likely to get abused because that is where the fan base comes from and that is the sort of vibe in the stands.

"I think lower down from that we are sometimes criticised for not having done enough with parks football and that has been a crucial issue for us.

That has been an area where it is far more difficult to get down to the players. There are very many layers at this level. There are the County FAs and the leagues and then there are the clubs. That has been a more difficult area of campaign but again I think what we try to do is to challenge the County FAs, the governing bodies at that level, to bring up their standards. It is difficult just because of the nature of the individuals involved. There is a real need for more work to be done there."

Ultimately, though, it is black players themselves who can do much in terms of football's race relations. Ironically it took a Frenchman playing in England to be abused by a Spaniard for the successful Nike driven 'Stand Up, Speak Up' campaign to get under way.

Arsenal and France icon Thierry Henry was fed up being abused and decided to initiate an interlocking black and white wristband in order to let the football fraternity and the general public know that black and white could work together.

Sadly, while the campaign, endorsed by megastars such as Ronaldinho and Ruud Van Nistelrooy, was well-intentioned it became just as much about the fashionable wristbands as the players uniting behind one message.

Henry's campaign started after Spain coach Luis Aragones was fined three thousand euros (two thousand and sixty pounds sterling) for racist remarks made about him in 2004. The Spanish Football Federation at first declined to take action against Aragones, but was then requested to do so by Spain's anti-violence commission.

Aragones called Henry "a black shit" when talking to the Arsenal striker's club colleague Jose Reyes but he insisted his comment was meant to motivate the

Spanish player, by comparing him favourably with Henry, and was not intended to be offensive.

"I never intended to offend anyone, and for that reason I have a very easy conscience," the Spanish manager said. "I'm obliged to motivate my players to get the best results. As part of that job, I use colloquial language, with which we can all understand each other within the framework of the football world."

Aragones has apologised publicly to Henry, although not personally, for any offence caused by his comments, which were captured by a television crew. The Spanish Football Federation also apologised formally.

The size of the fine was attacked by anti-racism campaigners. Kick It Out spokesman Leon Mann said: "We expected very little from the Spanish Football Association and are not surprised by this pitiful fine. The only positive is there's finally been a recognition that what Aragones said was racist, despite his protests.

"Questions have to be asked as to why the fine was only three thousand euros when it took such a lengthy process to get to this decision, and why someone found guilty of a racist comment is still in a job. Imagine what would have happened if Sven Goran Eriksson had come out and said the same."

Kick It Out believes racism is a problem in Spain. "The situation in Spanish football at the moment is desperate," added Mann.

Kick It Out has worked in tandem with some of black football's true pioneers in the hope that today's

Premiership heroes also understand the need for them to stand up and speak up.

Powar says: "Part of what we do is not just to say that racism is wrong. That is always the message, but sometimes that is too crude a message so we have to say look at the contribution these guys have made. We tell fans their club would not be what it is without people like this.

"People will respect legends of the game sometimes more than the current players because they are out of the daily hurly-burly. So it is useful to point out that Viv Anderson was the first black football full international to play for England and to explore some of the issues on it.

"The same with the so-called 'Three Degrees'. It's great for Cyrille and Brendon to talk about their experiences. It is the whole thing about generations and legacies.

"It's interesting you know, because I think there are some players now who take for granted that they will be given equal opportunities, that they will not be abused on the football pitch. They have heard the stories. They know that the moment they hear anything of a racist nature they are going to report it to someone or another. And I think that is as important as what goes on behind the scenes, what goes on in a dressing room.

"I think we have heard the stories about what people have faced on the training field, which is different from what happens during a match on a Saturday afternoon. You know; the way the coaches relate to them and crude things that are said to them by colleagues. Now I can't imagine that Jermain Defoe or Ashley Cole, or people of that ilk, are suffering level of abuse."

Powar has nothing but praise for black players' mental fortitude, both past and present. They have dealt with the subject of racism with their heads held high.

"Certainly the pioneers had no choice. If they were to walk off the field of play, or if they showed signs of weakness for want of a better way of putting it, then I think it would have been seen as a set back for them because they would have been seen as not prepared to put in the graft that was required.

"Wharton and Tull, for example, suffered particularly at the time when people were putting up with all sorts of things in factories and workplaces and schools and all that kind of stuff.

"Now I think it is the opposite. I think some of our players owe it to what's gone before and to future generations to say 'hang on a minute. This is 2005. If this happens to me I am off. I am going to withdraw my labour or I am going to raise this complaint at the highest level and pursue it with the vigilance that it deserves.'

"You don't always have to walk off. There are other ways of raising the issue. We talk to some players when it is clear they have come across a problem in their club that they think is to do with race and they have been aggressive in dealing with that, whether it is to do with the coach, the chief executive or the way someone has treated them. And those are the sort of players that we think in 2005 don't have to just sit back and take any of it.

"We know that football is a cosy culture. We know that there is that sense of the team comes first. Your personal concerns must come second regardless of that identity. Race is such a big issue to people that they need to step outside of that.

"I think the issue in Europe is a huge one. I think by the nature of this whole thing, by the nature of this problem we know, that sometimes things come in phases. I think we have made some very solid gains in England, but I would not trust that at some point those gains wouldn't come unravelled in some way. We might see for whatever reason for example fewer black British players making it great at the top level. It is easy to do that.

"I think the problem in Europe is that European nations are just not up with the debate in the way that we are in this country. They have not been through a Stephen Lawrence."

"They haven't had the largest police force being accused of institutional racism, they don't understand those sort of concepts of a group of people who are discriminated against, a section of the population discriminated against. They relate to their former colonies in different ways."

Stephen Lawrence was an eighteen-year-old sixth form student who was stabbed to death in Eltham, south London, on the night of 22 April, 1993. It soon became clear that his murder was motivated by racism. The racist murder of Lawrence was hardly unique – the Institute of Race Relations has documented twenty-four racially motivated murders in Britain since 1991. Controversy still surrounds many of these killings and the inadequacies of subsequent police operations, but it was the Stephen Lawrence case which has caught the public eye and the media's attention. This is because the police failed to bring successful charges against five youths, Jamie and Neil Acourt, Gary Dobson,

David Norris and Luke Knight, who were viewed as the prime suspects in the murder.

It has taken two police inquiries, a public inquiry, and the Macpherson Report, to reveal the extent of the corruption and the conscious and unconscious racism that afflicted the police force investigating Stephen Lawrence's murder.

If Powar and his colleagues were put out of work it would mean that racism in football has been buried. That sadly will never be the case as long as broader society suffers from the same ills. But the hope at the campaign is that progress continues.

> "I think two things need to happen. One is that you have to maintain a message. It might be that it is a more subtle message or it might be that the ownership of that message is entirely with the clubs, although there is a trust issue there. Some clubs will just move on and forget that there was ever a problem and not really maintain it in a way that is positive.
>
> "Then I think there are specific problems that need to be addressed and people need to have pressure continually put on them. And then there is the issue of the lower leagues and amateur football. To some extent we have deferred action on the issue of abuse at those clubs. We now trust that the clubs which have a problem will be able to deal with it in their own way because they should have the steward training packs. They should have the advice and guidance from us. They know how to get a message out.
>
> "They have the policing and the educational stuff and that knowledge should be with them now. We have standards now and it is important because we have got a situation now where clubs

are getting competitive in trying to achieve it. The very basic level of that is for people to understand how to deal with racial abuse. So we have to, in many ways, say 'look you need to deal with it. It is your club where the problem arises and you need to understand exactly how to respond".

But brighter times are ahead, according to Powar and his team:

"That is the way we are heading at the moment. I see no reason why we couldn't get there. I guess what gives me that optimism is that I have been to the United States and I have seen progress over there. The States has as many race problems as anywhere else but within the sporting field you do not get fans abusing black athletes.

"You look at the other side in Europe, the way that the abuse of black athletes is still so much a part of the culture in the way that it was once here. We are positioned more towards the US.

"I think we will get there at some point. It depends on how wide race relations goes and it depends on what happens and there is a complexity to all of these things but that has to be our ultimate objective, that black footballers can play football without abuse."

One of the most significant developments in the long and often turbulent history of black footballers in Britain took place in 1993. Paul Ince became the first black player to captain the senior England team when they played United States.

Ince might have got the captain's armband only because of the absence of David Platt but a black footballer leading the national side was a pivotal moment in the history of black footballers.

Sol Campbell, who made his name at Tottenham but had his glory years at near neighbours Arsenal, has also led the national side. He made his debut against the Republic of Ireland in February 1995 at just twenty-years-old. After that he established himself as a pivotal member of England's defence in much the same way that Des Walker had before him.

Indeed Campbell was many people's choice of captain when another Arsenal legend, Tony Adams, announced his international retirement in October 2000. However, the armband was eventually to be given to Alan Shearer.

Ince leading out the national side meant that black footballers had well and truly arrived.

In simple terms, the England football team belongs to the people. The indigenous people. That much was made clear as many of the early black players who pulled on the famous white shirt discovered.

Regis, Blissett, Barnes and Mark Chamberlain took enormous grief while wearing the Three Lions in the 1980s. So for a black player to be deemed good enough to actually captain the team was a significant breakthrough. It was acceptance at the highest level.

It was fitting that Ince, the self-styled 'Guvnor', should receive that accolade. Ince was spotted by West Ham coach John Lyall as a precocious twelve-year-old, and signed for the East London club as a YTS trainee at fourteen. In 1985 he was offered professional terms.

While Clyde Best was sometimes a figure of fun during his own time at Upton Park, Ince was to almost immediately gain the respect of the club's notoriously demanding supporters.

After serving the club with distinction for four seasons, making seventy-two appearances while hitting four goals, Ince was to move into the big time with a controversial £1million transfer to Manchester United in September 1989.

The West Ham supporters' feelings for Ince dissipated once he was seen with a Manchester United shirt on the back page of a daily newspaper even before he had sealed his move to Old Trafford.

However, Ince, a tough, ball-winning midfielder, was on his way to becoming one of the best anchormen in the business. In many ways he was similar in style to Remi Moses, another outstanding black midfielder who graced Old Trafford prior to 'The Guvnor's' reign.

In six seasons at Old Trafford, Ince was an integral part of the United side built by Sir Alex Ferguson which finally, after many years of heartbreak and disappointment, won the championship in the 1992-93 season. On occasion Ince would lead United too.

After winning the FA Cup in 1990, Ince was to win the League Cup in 1992, though that season was ultimately to end in disappointment as arch-rivals Leeds United pipped the Manchester side to the championship.

As Manchester United were on their way to dominating the English game, Ince was carving out an awesome reputation. Not too long ago black players were labelled as unable to get involved in the sometimes brutal physicality of the English game. That accusation could never be levelled at Ince, who appeared to thrive on the game's mental and physical demands.

In the centre of midfield he dictated play and would very often be seen shouting and cajoling his teammates. It is said that Sir Alex Ferguson often bought players in his own feisty image and his eventual falling out with Ince was probably a case of two bulls attempting to live in the same field.

To truly understand Ince's value to Manchester United during an illustrious career is to acknowledge that the player who replaced him as the heartbeat of the Old Trafford club was a certain Irishman called Roy Keane.

Ince helped Manchester United to their first Double in 1993-94 and went on to win every domestic honour available and a European Cup Winners' medal in 1991.

In total, Ince gained 53 England caps, the first of which came while at United. His international career spanned seven years and five managers and he played in the 1998 World Cup and two European Championships, 1996 and 2000.

Ince's Old Trafford career was cut short by his famous falling out with Sir Alex, who always looked to shuffle his cards to maintain success. While Ince was surprisingly transferred to Inter Milan in June 1995 for £7million, Sir Alex was replacing his midfield with fresh legs in the shape of future England internationals Nicky Butt, David Beckham and Paul Scholes.

Ince's Italian sojourn ended with a transfer to Liverpool before he went on to revive the fortunes of Middlesbrough and Wolverhampton Wanderers who he helped back into football's big time in 2003.

Any team with Paul Ince in it benefited from his will to win and tenacity. Patrick Vieira and Claude Makelele have been lauded for their midfield contributions to Arsenal, Chelsea Real Madrid and France but Ince can be considered the original 'Guvnor'.

Chapter 13

Hope Powell

WHILE Paul Ince's role as captain of England did so much for the advance of black players, so too did the appointment of Hope Powell to the position of England women's national coach.

The progress of black footballers has not been confined to the strides made by the men. Hope Powell has not only been a shining light as a player, having played the game at the highest level, but in 1998 she was chosen to lead the burgeoning women's game in England.

Not only was Powell the first woman and the youngest coach to manage an England side, but also the first black woman.

She remembers her feelings on hearing the news of her appointment. "I think I experienced every emotion. I was overwhelmed at first. It was very exciting but a bit scary too. Then I thought 'this is a once in a lifetime opportunity, I've got to do it!'

"Being young, female and black I knew I could be a positive role model for young people. I hope I can help some young black people in particular to believe in themselves and strive to be the best. I want to succeed for myself and, as the first black player in such a senior position, I want to do it for everyone else as well."

Powell is one of the most respected figures at the FA's Soho Square headquarters in London. She has the task of overseeing almost every aspect of the women's game in England. Her love affair with the game, however, was to start in the early 1970s during the football's biggest showcase, the World Cup.

"I don't know if it's my earliest, but my fondest memory that made me want to play football even more would have been the 1974 World Cup. I just remember Peru being in this World Cup.

"It was just the whole thing. I could appreciate the atmosphere on telly. I was very young, it just looked fantastic and I wanted to be there.

"It was everything to me at the time. It made me want to play the game. I remember kids playing football in the park that summer – and I was one of those Peruvian players. I was at the World Cup playing in the park! It was brilliant and that was the fondest memory for me."

Having had her appetite whetted as an eight-year-old, Powell was to get more serious about the game at the age of eleven. Her local club Millwall Lionesses was the starting point for a career that, had she been a man, would have seen her become one of the iconic names in top flight football.

"I used to play street football with my brothers, but I started playing organised football by chance really. I wasn't always accepted, because I was a girl. I was the smallest but I kept coming back when I played street football.

"Someone at my school was going to Millwall, so I went along and I enjoyed it so much that I just kept going back. Millwall was always well known for women's football. It really surprised me that so many girls played football.

"And that's how it started. And then from there I

was invited back on the Sunday to play. I didn't support Millwall. I liked Chelsea at the time. I remember Ray Wilkins; I thought his legs were fabulously athletics. But all I really wanted to do was play and Millwall gave me that opportunity."

Even at that tender age, Powell was ambitious. She would go on to gain 66 England caps. But the classy midfielder knew that representing her country was her destiny.

"At eleven years of age, when I found out there was an international side, I knew I would play for them. I got that feeling because I knew I was better than anybody else. So I thought if I was better than all the girls I am playing with I must be able to get into the team.

"It was not a case of being arrogant. It was something you knew was your ambition. It's like when you work hard in life, in a job and you want to succeed in something that is what I wanted to do. I wanted to play football.

"The biggest thing I wanted to do was earn a living, so that was why I went into coaching. I wanted to get paid for it. Purely monetary. Some people think about giving things back, no, I wanted to earn money."

Like so many young people with a West Indian background, Powell had to overcome her mother's diffidence towards football. In the 1970s education was the priority for West Indian parents as playing football was alien to the community, and was never seen as a serious career prospect.

"When I first went to Millwall my friend's parents took me. My mum didn't allow me to go. I went but I got back quite late and I wasn't going again as far as my mum was concerned. But as far as I was concerned I was going!

"There was no way I was not going. And my mum was strict, a typical West Indian. It wouldn't happen in this day and age but the belt would come out and stuff like that. But I was going to football regardless.

"My mother's culture is a very different culture so it was a bit difficult for her to understand why a girl would want to play football. It doesn't happen in Jamaica. Now she is quite proud, especially after I got the England job and there was so much media coverage.

"It's really funny because sometimes I wonder if she really understands the game and maybe I don't give her enough credit. Now mum will go 'how you getting on and who you playing, did you win?'

"If we don't win it's because the players are not eating enough rice and peas and she comes back with all of that but I know she has got a scrap book which she tells me about, although I have never seen it.

"I just think it is sweet. She follows football on TV. She came to the Euros but I am not the sort of person who is, for want of a word, a bragger. It is a job and that is what I do for a living. The other bits are a bonus."

While happy to be a role model to young people – "I think it is important if it is positive and I know it positive so that is good. I am happy with that" – Powell is less enamoured with life as a woman in a male-dominated sport.

"Although I have got the highest coaching qualification in the world people still look at me as a female and probably don't give me the credit a man would have. It makes me laugh. I don't know if you have experienced things where people talk about the game and they are clueless? Yes, they talk a good game.

"I sit in technical meetings with guys and they are all very knowledgeable and I listen more, and I learn a lot from listening. Whereas a lot of guys want to tell you what they know and I find it quite comical.

"The biggest issue is the fact that I am a female. If I was a man with sixty-six caps and thirty-five goals, and had managed England for seven years it would be different but I am a female in a male world.

"I am very cool and calm and I have done as much work as anybody else. Actually no, that is a lie I have done more as a woman. I had to go and do my Pro-License. I wanted to prove a point. We worked in groups and I wanted our group to be the best. I pulled my group together and they gave me credit for it. They couldn't do it, they went off on a tangent. I wanted to be successful because I didn't want to be seen as a token gesture. I bloody worked hard for that Pro-License. I worked my arse off as did everybody else. But I know that I pulled that group together."

As the women's game grows in popularity, as England hosting Euro 2005 proved, there is the threat that the women's game could suffer the same ills as the men's game.

While black male footballers have been consistently targeted, Powell and other black women have escaped to a degree. Is that because to the morons they provide less of a threat than black men?

That said, Powell still recalls with horror her own experiences. "I remember one game when I was quite young and someone referred to me as a 'black bastard' or something of that nature. Luckily one of my teammates heard and she went absolutely berserk – she was five years older than me. What she did was good otherwise I think we would have had a punch up. I didn't like it. I was not happy.

"The second occasion was when I was playing for England against Croatia and I pulled my hamstring right near the tunnel. The physio came on and we decided I should go and shower because obviously I couldn't play any more. As I was walking down the tunnel this young boy, no more than twelve, made a Nazi salute at me. I was shocked, I couldn't believe it. I think I just smiled. It was like 'Jesus you are too young to even be going there.' So that was really the only other time."

Like so many of her male counterparts, Powell would rather focus on football matters as opposed to race issues. They exist, but looking forward rather than back is her philosophy.

"I don't even think about it. I don't think about race, I don't think about colour, I just think about the players. If it was to happen, if someone was being racially abusive within the camp, I wouldn't have it. It wouldn't happen. They would be gone. When they are playing on the pitch, I can't influence that. I have no control but it doesn't even enter my head, I just want them to play football.

181

"I think the crowds help our game. There are children, lots of females. It's a friendlier environment. We are trying to create that sort of atmosphere, so that helps. In terms of the people that drive the game, they are young, educated and can see beyond colour. When I am in that environment with my team – not the players but my staff – it is not even an issue and that is nice. There has never been an issue. Not once. Never.

"If you're in a club or a team you need to find someone to talk to about it like the manager or coach" is Powell's advice to anyone that suffers simply because of the colour of their skin.

"If it was me, I would always say something. But under no circumstances give up [football]. Don't allow small-minded people to force you to give up something you love."

As national coach, Powell not only manages the senior women's team, she also oversees the Under-19s, Under-17s and under-15s development pool and the National Player Development Centre based at Loughborough University, as well as implementing a female coach mentoring scheme.

In 2002, she received an OBE from the Queen at Buckingham Palace, due reward for some thirty years in football.

While her Royal appointment must have been one of the highlights of a great career, leading the host nation during Euro 2005 also filled the modest Powell with pride.

Powell put a brave face on England's early exit from a major tournament but the fact that it was staged on home turf and screened on the BBC made her proud. And her role as women's football figurehead is set to leave a legacy that the forthcoming generations can benefit from.

There were 25,694 in the City of Manchester Stadium as England kicked off Euro 2005 against Finland on a Sunday evening, a testimony to Powell and her team and background staff's hard work. Just under 70,000 watched England's three games. During BBC TV's broadcast of England's game in Manchester an amazing 2.9 million people were said to be watching at home.

Having been in post for nearly a decade Powell wants to leave something tangible behind. "I think from a playing perspective it would be from developing the game and moving it forward and playing the game the way I feel it should be played, which is I believe

"I want everybody to be able to play football. Play it on the deck. Flair, I want it to be natural and free flowing in terms of the football. I think for everybody on the outside, people that come to watch the game, it has to be entertaining and just basically move the whole game forward and give players the opportunity.

"The girls were magnificent during Euro 2005. I would argue with anyone that said differently. I think we've won over some of our critics. We've proved we can compete with the best in the world. There were so many positives to take out of the tournament to mention.

"I want the game to be played the right way. I want players to play with a free spirit and not be afraid. And more importantly to enjoy it and certainly have structure. We have strategies, this is how they are going to play, this is how we have to play and make it more player centred. I want all my players to be free, like the Brazilians. You can see

183

it, can't you? You can see that the Brazilians just play with a free spirit and I like that. That is what I would like my team to emulate.

"I think women's football is something that is still developing. I think there is lots of work to be done – that excites me. Young kids that are coming through that are so talented and to play a part in their development I would like to do that. Coach education, educate and more specifically women. To attract more female coaches into the game also appeals to me."

Chapter 14

The influence of Sven

IN 2001 Sven Goran Eriksson became the first 'foreigner' to take charge of the England national team. It was a bold move by his employers, the Football Association, considering the history of the game in England.

At best the Swede's appointment was treated with disdain. A fine coaching career in Europe was all well and good and indicated that he was, at the time, the best man for the job but there was a problem; he was not English. Eriksson was to suffer from some of the same prejudices that black footballers have endured for decades: distrust.

Eriksson began his coaching career in 1979 in his native Sweden with IFK Gothenburg. His side were to twice win the Swedish Cup and win the UEFA Cup, before he was head-hunted by Portuguese outfit Benfica.

The astute Swede confirmed his credentials as a top class coach when Benfica won the League title, losing just one game, although they lost to Anderlecht in the UEFA Cup. From there he went to Roma, Florence and another sojourn at Benfica. This saw his stock rise before he really made his name with two more Serie A teams, Sampdoria and Lazio.

Having survived the publication of lurid details about his sex life, including affairs with TV celebrity Ulrikka Jonsson and FA employee Faria Alam – and some dodgy results along the way – the Swede, having been suitably bashed, led England to yet another

World Cup even though he apologised after the team went out at the quarter-final stage.

He might not have played with any black players during his own playing days with home town club Torsby United but his long management CV meant that eventually he would work with black footballers.

He recalls: "It must have been in Portugal in 1982 when I became the manager of Benfica. They had a lot of black players especially coming from Brazil but also from Angola.

"They have a long experience of black players from that country. If you remember Eusebio, he came when he was a teenager so it has always been between Africa, definitely Mozambique, Angola and other ex-colonies to Portugal. At a certain time clubs were allowed to have a Brazilian player. They were not counted like foreigners so during my five years in Portugal racists were never an issue."

During his time at Sampdoria, from 1992-1997, Eriksson worked with Des Walker, a player who had done so much to destroy some of the stereotypes of black players. Yes, he was lightning quick over the ground, but he would always relish a tackle in his role as centre-half.

Under Eriksson's brief tutelage, Walker flourished and proved to be the one of the first black players to come off the 'Centre Half Production Line' which has subsequently produced the likes of Paul Elliott, Sol Campbell, Rio Ferdinand, Wes Brown, Ledley King and Zat Knight to name just a few.

The former England manager does not have time for those who judge people or individuals by race or colour.

The influence of Sven

While slightly surprised by some of the race-in-football issues in England, Eriksson admits there was an even bigger problem in Italy.

"Yes, I have been surprised by some of the issues over here a little bit because you have a lot of black people in this country. You had colonies, so it was a little bit surprising, but unfortunately I was used to it because one of the clubs I had in Italy was Lazio and we had a big problem.

"I don't know how many, but some matches you would have maybe one thousand who more or less every time were booing the black players and it was poor. We tried very hard to stop it and on occasions we were fined."

He was fully behind his black players in the England team who were so shamefully racially abused by Spanish supporters in a not so friendly international in 2004.

"At first I didn't understand what they were doing but after some minutes you recognised what was happening and of course sitting there – on the bench – you can't do very much about it.

"Then there was a big discussion after the game, should the manager take the players off and things like that. In a friendly game it doesn't matter that much but I don't think you can do that in qualification games for a World Cup. I was wondering what would have happened if I had taken the players off.

"What can you do? You can talk afterwards to the press and try to give messages that this shouldn't happen. I think the players were not very happy at all. Absolutely not. Their heads were down in the dressing room afterwards.

"Of course, I can understand that. I mean it is a terrible situation with people booing at you. I can understand if you make an own goal or whatever but not because of the colour of your skin. Absolutely not."

For days afterwards the world's press took the line that the abuse of the players was so bad that they could, if not should, have left the field of play. Many suggested that by voting with their feet the players would have sent a clear message of intent to those that attend football matches with the sole intention of racially abusing black players. Others implied that to walk would have been a moral victory for the bigots.

But the abuse was so bad that to have walked off the field, in full view of a captive audience, would and could have had a telling effect. One international captain told me that if it had been his team he would have taken the players off. These types of incidents always generate debate but what is not up for discussion is that the players abused are always black and always will be and they should be protected.

What was in no doubt, however, was the fact that where the talk of progress in terms of anti-racism campaigns in football is concerned there is still an awful lot of work to do.

For the black player suffering from such torrid abuse, the only difference between those who discredited football in the past and those who do the same thing now, is that they impart their invective to a much bigger audience – such is the surfeit of TV and radio broadcasters covering the game. And it has the ability to expose them.

Chapter 15

All Wright

ONE PLAYER, MORE than any other, propelled the black footballer into the hearts and minds of the football fraternity, both black and white, in the 1980s. Ian Wright, with his penchant for goals and his effervescent personality, did as much for the black footballer in that decade as Paul Ince and Sol Campbell who both captained the full England side.

Wright entered the public consciousness because his was a true rags to riches story. A late starter in the professional game, Wright went from non-league football to TV stardom in almost no time at all.

Along the way he made football acceptable to a whole new generation of black football fans. With Wrighty at the helm, football became cool for the black community. He was an urban hero to whom the youngsters on the street could relate.

After rejections from Millwall and Brighton, he played for amateur and non-league sides, while working as a labourer and plasterer, culminating with a spell at Greenwich Borough, where he was spotted by Crystal Palace scout Peter Prentice.

The South London club, nicknamed the Eagles, were to soar for a while after signing Wright in 1985 as an ambitious twenty-two-year-old. He was to score consistently as he made a name for himself, one of the many highlights coming during the 1990 FA Cup Final against Manchester United at Wembley. His goal-scoring partner was the more languid Mark Bright. They formed an irresistible partnership which saw them go on to bigger and better things as individuals.

In that final, which ended 3-3, Wright, who had been doubtful with injury before the game, truly hit the big time by coming off the substitute's bench and scoring two stunning goals. These goals, as well as the cheeky-chappie manner in which he played the game, endeared him to most supporters and introduced him to the cup final's traditionally huge audience.

This display resulted in him being bought by Arsenal in 1991 for £2.5million, at the time the record fee for the Highbury club. It proved to be money well spent for both parties.

Wright, who proved that he could make the step up in class without losing the essence of his personality, scored on his debut against Leicester City in a League Cup tie and followed up by bagging a hat-trick on his League debut against Southampton. Hans Christian Andersen would have loved the story so far.

While the goals flowed, there could be no denying that Wright, even under the dull but successful regime of George Graham, made Arsenal a magnet for the black community. Here was an ordinary guy making good in a place seen as dangerous to many in the black community. Wright's success made Highbury a relatively safe haven for black football fans who were now prepared to part with their hard earned cash and attend matches despite the obvious racism on the terraces and streets surrounding so many football clubs.

There had been black players at Highbury before – for instance Paul Davis, David Rocastle and Michael Thomas – but they did not attract black fans in the same numbers as Wright.

All Wright

So just what made Wright so universally popular? In short, he gave fans what they wanted; he was a trier. Not too many games would go by with the diminutive Wright giving less than one hundred per cent effort and in the days of inflated, almost disgusting salaries, fans wanted maximum effort from their heroes as a minimum.

They got that from Wright and loved him for it. He even got away with outrageous tackles on opponents and all manner of disciplinary problems because, in the main, he wore his heart on his sleeve.

He appealed to black youngsters because he wanted to express himself while playing football and would also stand up for himself when the need arose. Many within the Asian and black communities heard Wright speak up long before Thierry Henry's anti-racism campaign was launched in 2005.

Wright was born to play for Arsenal if only because his place of birth was the Royal Military Hospital in Woolwich, London, which was where Royal Arsenal were formed in 1886.

Goals simply flowed for a player who could play the game with a smile or a snarl. In 1993 he became the quickest Arsenal player to score one hundred goals for the club, beating Ted Drake's forty year record.

By the time that Arsène Wenger arrived at Highbury in 1996, Wright's sensational top flight career was thought unlikely to get any better – but try telling him that!

Despite being in his early thirties, he continued to find the back of the net and in September 1997, fittingly in front of the Highbury faithful, he broke another goal-scoring record.

In glorious sunshine, Wright scored a hat-trick to beat Cliff Bastin's all-time Arsenal goal-scoring record.

The celebration that greeted his third goal on that memorable afternoon was a sight to behold.

He pulled his jersey over his head to uncover a T-shirt adorned by the figure '179' (the goals he had accumulated). His beaming smile will never be forgotten by anyone who witnessed his elation as he put Bolton Wanderers to the sword.

That smile was followed up in May 1998 when Wenger's rampant Arsenal claimed the Premiership on the way to another Double. Everton were the victims this time as Wright collected his Premiership winners' medal; his face quite lit up Highbury that Sunday evening.

Wright was everybody's hero. Even opposing fans applauded either his outstanding goals or novel goal celebrations which would generally involve the supporters.

Wright was without question the most influential player of his generation. He gives the credit for his own career to the pioneers who played in isolation on the football field and had to take the abuse with no support system to protect them. "Garth Crooks, Laurie Cunningham, Cyrille Regis, Pele and Kevin Keegan were my heroes.

> "Keegan was my biggest one out of all of them, obviously the rest because they were black. They were in the limelight and you'd say 'God they've made it.' They were the ones who made me want to be a footballer."

As with most footballers, injuries took their toll on Wright. Hamstring problems were to blight the latter part of his career.

In the summer of 1998, he moved to West Ham United but he spent less than a season with the

Hammers. There were short spells with Nottingham Forest, Celtic and Burnley before he hung up his boots in 2000, the year he was the unassuming subject of *This Is Your Life* in January 2000. It was reported that the show was watched by nearly 10 million viewers.

The norm for footballers once they had called it a day used to be several rounds of golf or to open a pub. Wright was having none of that! Having dabbled with TV since January 1998, he signed a two year deal with the BBC in 2001 to present a number of projects.

Friends Like These and *Ian Wright – Surviving The Kalahari*, a show in which he survived two nights on his own in one of the world's most inhospitable deserts, were both considered successes on the small screen.

But it was the late night *Friday Night's All Wright* which really cemented Wright's cult hero status. Here was an ex-player who had moved seamlessly from a football dressing room to a TV dressing room with minimum effort.

On TV he was everything he had been on the football field; charming, competent and determined to do well for himself and ultimately the community from which he came.

Most would have thought that Wright would delve into his little black book and come up with a long list of footballers to appear on his show. But, as ever, he did things with panache.

Among his high profile guests were Elton John, Will Smith, Westlife and Denzel Washington. The show ran for two seasons and if Wright was popular during his playing career, the top-rated show meant his popularity was now off the Richter Scale. He gained a host of new admirers, including members of the opposite sex who were captivated by his silky smooth charm allied to natural presence.

He was to receive his MBE for football achievement and whenever the charismatic Wright talks about his playing days he's as direct as he was when bearing down on the opponents' goal.

Of his early days in non-league football, Wright says: "The local leagues are terrible because you're talking about older guys, big belly guys, slow guys and people like myself. You'd get these comments – black bastard and nigger – all that stuff when you were playing against them.

> "When I was at Crystal Palace, in the early days I experienced racism from the older, senior professionals. At the time it was quite disturbing. I didn't want to be there. I had a decent job then, it was in my early days and a phase where I wanted to give up. But I had good people round me who said 'You can't give up just because of that or they'll have won.'"

When asked whether he had experienced more racism since he had become famous, Wright adds: "I think with jealous people it's the easiest thing in the world to say a racist comment to a black player. I used to get a load of bad letters, I didn't read them all of them as they distressed me. Those people are just sick, I haven't done anything to them so I just say to myself that they are just stupid, ignorant people.

> "I couldn't even imagine what it would have been like in Cyrille Regis' and Laurie Cunningham's day because I couldn't have taken it. But I suppose it was harder for them to speak out then – and that is why I'd now take any opportunity to speak that I can.
> "People aren't tolerating it any more, and that will filter through. It's always going to be problem

in society though. You'll just find it'll get really isolated at some stage. By the time my boy Stacy gets older I think it'll be really old hat."

Wright's great friend John Barnes once jokingly described himself as Martin Luther King while firebrand Wright was Malcolm X.

Of two iconic black American leaders, Wright admits:

"Malcolm X could have been a great leader for us – a real inspirational man. He did wrong when he was younger, but he came through that and then he went into a real radical black movement. When he went to Mecca and came back he realised that everybody should be together. Then he would have been the man to lead not only black people but everybody, but he got shot.

"I like Martin Luther King's preaching, it's quite inspirational, but I feel he was more pacifying. You can't just turn the other cheek, that's why when Malcolm X said 'by any means necessary' – if you do this to me I'm going to do this to you – I thought it was a better way.

"You can't expect somebody, when they're being shot at, to hit them back with a sponge or something. You've got to do what you've got to do."

Chapter 16

The Strike Partnership

IAN WRIGHT WAS one of many black high class goal-scorers in the English game. But the two whose goals were rewarded with football's biggest prizes were Andrew Cole and Dwight Yorke of Manchester United.

The partnership between Cole and Yorke proved sensational while they were at Old Trafford. It was a strange pairing; Cole, a moody, brooding character found that Yorke, who truly played with a smile on his face, was his perfect partner. In fact, the pair hit it off immediately when Yorke joined Cole at the Theatre of Dreams in 1998. Their goals were to prove pivotal to the club's Treble-winning season in 1999 which culminated in European Cup glory against Bayern Munich.

The fact they were both successful at arguably the biggest club in the world was testimony to how far black footballers had come since the lack of recognition given to the likes of Albert Johanneson just thirty years previous at Leeds.

Manchester United have always had famous goal poachers but none of them had helped the club to a Treble.

Cole, who was then known simply as Andy but who now prefers to be called Andrew, was the first to arrive in the north west of England. In January 1995 Alex Ferguson paid Newcastle United a then British record transfer fee of £6.2million for a player who started his career at Arsenal before moving to Bristol City.

After joining Newcastle United in March 1993 he was an instant hero with the Toon Army, helping Newcastle secure promotion to the Premier League in his first season. The following year, his 34 league goals won him the 'European Golden Boot' award and the 1994 Young Player of the Year title.

He went a long way in changing the attitude of Newcastle's fans who were as racially minded as many other football fans in the north of England.

Having narrowly missed out on a Premiership medal in his first season with Manchester United, Cole won the league with 1995-96. Although one consolation during that near-miss season for Cole was the five goals he scored as United crushed hapless Ipswich Town 9-0 in the Premiership's record victory.

But even though Cole helped United to many honours, he was still maligned in the press because he missed chances. As such his England career suffered because of the distrust England managers had of him, none more so than Glenn Hoddle who had a famous falling out with the striker before a major tournament.

But it was the arrival of the charismatic Yorke, and his subsequent almost telepathic relationship with Cole that was to set Old Trafford buzzing. United manager Alex Ferguson had acquired Yorke's services after admitting that of all the strikers that his club had faced over the years, Yorke had been the biggest thorn in his side. A case of better the devil you know!

Even though the progress of black footballers was moving quickly in the late 1990s the sight of two black strikers leading the line at the most famous club in the world was almost like arriving at the promised land for black players and fans. Who could blame the pioneers if they had thrown envious glances at Old Trafford? Cole and Yorke had it all for a while; fame, fortune and success.

Yorke's arrival at Old Trafford was preceded by a real Caribbean fairytale. African footballers have long since cemented their talents in English, Continental and world football but hardly any players from the Caribbean had made an impact before Yorke arrived from Trinidad & Tobago with his languid style and toothy grin.

Yorke was discovered by the then Aston Villa manager Graham Taylor during the Birmingham club's tour to the West Indies. He cost his new employers just £120,000. They were to make a huge profit when he moved to United for £12.6million in 1998.

One of nine children, legend has it that the young Yorke spent his formative football years playing barefoot. His first pair of boots came courtesy of catching crabs to earn pocket money.

It was not Taylor but Dr Jozef Venglos who gave Yorke his full league debut for Villa, against, ironically, Manchester United. It was not long before Yorke – a close friend of another Caribbean phenomenon, cricketer Brian Lara, who also played in Birmingham with Warwickshire – was making a name for himself in the second city.

The goals arrived with regularity but Yorke proved to be more ambitious than the club. The season before he left Villa, however, he helped them clinch a place in the UEFA Cup. The club's top scorer with sixteen goals in total in all competitions, Yorke found the net in the season's final fixture, a crucial 1-0 win over champions Arsenal.

During his heyday at Villa, the Holte End would sing: "Start spreading the news, he's playing today, I want to see him score again, Dwight Yorke, Dwight Yorke," sung to the tune of the Frank Sinatra classic *New York, New York.*

What would a Clyde Best, and others, have thought of the affection shown to Yorke? Most of what the early, pioneering black footballers heard was abuse.

Yorke's popularity was another massive step forward for the black footballer, in many ways similar to the love shown to Ian Wright at Highbury. To endorse the fact that Yorke had Villa's fans eating out of his hands he was voted Player of the Year for two successive seasons, an honour not bestowed on too many players.

The young Yorke was tempted to head back to sunnier climes when he first arrived at Villa as a wide-eyed teenager; such was his early anxiety in England. Villa and United must be pleased he stayed.

"I didn't know exactly what I was coming into. I did not know how things were going to work out. And, of course, the weather, the food, the people – it was different and it took a little while before I adjusted to it all. I'm pleased that I stuck it out."

Cricket has always been the Caribbean's number one pastime, even with the West Indian team's demise. But when Yorke made his multi-million pound move to United the repercussions reverberated not just in his native island but the region.

Yorke's move proved that with ability, dedication and vision all things were possible. His transfer to Old Trafford put cricket under pressure. A visit to the Caribbean will prove that. Replica shirts, whether from Manchester United, Liverpool, Chelsea or Arsenal, are a regular sight whether you are in Kingston, Bridgetown, Port of Spain or Castries.

With the cricket team still out of sorts, it is obvious why football has grown in popularity. Premiership matches can be watched at home while many bars and restaurants have bought satellite dishes with a view to giving locals, and, more importantly, tourists, the opportunity to watch the action. In short, Yorke's big money move to United made football an acceptable rival to cricket.

Yorke enjoyed a superb first season at Old Trafford when everything seemed to go right and the Treble was secured.

Many fans were fascinated by the rapport, both on and off the field, between Yorke and Cole. Many had thought Cole to be a loner, unable to establish a successful striking partnership.

The partnership brought the best out of both men. That 1998-99 season saw them score more than fifty goals with Yorke grabbing twenty-nine in all competitions.

Included were some truly magical moments. There was a scintillating hat-trick against Leicester City, a brace of stunning headers against Inter Milan, a deft chip over Chelsea 'keeper Ed de Goey, a last gasp equaliser against fierce rivals Liverpool in the FA Cup and, of course, that vital equaliser against Juventus in Turin which suggested that the European Cup was destined for Old Trafford that season.

Yorke's days at United were truly heady. It was thought that once Eric Cantona departed there would be a massive void at the club, yet Yorke was able to fill it. Teddy Sheringham could not assume Cantona's but Yorke, in tandem with Cole, managed it, however briefly.

His off-field antics, however, involving nightclubs and women, were to land him in hot water on more than one occasion which eventually led to a falling out with disciplinarian Ferguson.

He was excluded from the first team squad, making his move from Old Trafford a case of 'when' rather than 'if.' There was a feeling that if he could have disciplined himself, there was no telling what he could have achieved at United. But it was as if there was no other summit for him to climb after the win against Bayern Munich in Barecelona's Camp Nou on the ultimate European glory night in May 1999. Spells at Blackburn Rovers, Birmingham City and Sydney FC in Australia, were light years away from the drama and honours at Old Trafford. But what nobody can deny is that very much in the same way he took Aston Villa by storm, Yorke made, and left, his mark at the biggest club in the world.

In September 2006 Yorke attempted to restart his career in England by signing for Roy Keane at Sunderland.

Manchester United have long been known for producing star players, men like Best, Charlton, Law, Robson, Giggs and Beckham to name a few. And while he may have a little way to go before sitting comfortably in such exalted company, Rio Ferdinand has all the qualities to be an Old Trafford legend. And like most icons Ferdinand creates headlines for a mixture of reasons. Ferdinand is close to the top when a list of most influential black footballers of recent times is assembled.

A cousin of former England international Les and brother of Anton, currently a first-team player with West Ham United, Rio, as they say, comes from good stock.

The brothers were to come up against each other for the very first time in the top flight as West Ham entertained Manchester United at Upton Park on 27 November 2005.

It was not just a milestone occasion for the Ferdinand family. Just days before, George Best had lost his fight for life and his legendary status resulted in all those present at Upton Park that day replacing the traditional minute's silence with applause. The Ferdinand brothers will never forget the first time they came face to face in the Premiership.

There is no doubt that Rio – as classy a centre-half as there is the world – can play, but he has grabbed nearly as many off-field headlines, confirming that black footballers are very much part of the fabric of English football, whether that be good, bad or indifferent.

He has been banned from driving on four occasions – a total contrast with his on field disciplinary record. He still has not received a red card and bearing in mind the position he plays that is a near miracle. For a player whose job is to challenge and be involved at the heart of football's physical aspect, Ferdinand picks up only the occasional yellow card, such is his tackling ability allied to timing and confidence.

The days when cynics suggested that black players shied away from tackling, could not lead their teammates and could not lift their heads to make a telling pass have long gone and players such as Ferdinand are the reasons why.

Black footballers have a reputation for wanting to score goals coupled with fancy footwork to bemuse the opposition but Ferdinand's capabilities have made defending popular among young players who previously only wanted to play with panache and stick the ball in the back of the net.

Ferdinand's career started at West Ham United. The East London club have a decent track record of finding and developing young defenders with the iconic Bobby Moore, England's 1966 World Cup winning captain, the ultimate defender produced by the Hammers.

Ferdinand has turned out to be another elegant footballer who defends with intelligence and guile, while also attempting to use the ball intelligently when in possession.

Bob Hazell and George Berry were among the first notable black centre-halves. But their game was based on intimidatory tactics which did not readily allow them to show their football skills. While Hazell and Berry were artisans, Ferdinand has proved to be a real artist.

Ferdinand was to catch the eye of almost every major club in Europe with his smooth displays for the Hammers. The likes of Real Madrid and Barcelona were even said to be interested in the Peckham-born youngster. Surprisingly it was Leeds United who were prepared to stump up a staggering £18million, a world record fee for a defender and the British transfer record.

The move to Elland Road in November 2000 benefited Rio possibly more than the Yorkshire club. A combination of the high profile move and his subsequent imperious performances saw him claim a regular England spot. He had made his full international debut against Cameroon at Wembley in November 1997 and quickly established himself as one of England's first-choice centre-halves.

In July 2002, Ferdinand dealt Leeds a hammer blow by handing in a transfer request. He thought moving to Leeds would satisfy his ambitions but realised this was not the case. The result was a five year £29.3million contract with Leeds' deadly rivals Manchester United. He had played just seventy-three games for the Elland

Road club, who nevertheless made an £11million profit.

His move to Old Trafford has been blighted by Arsenal and Chelsea winning the Premiership and the furore created by his suspension for missing a drugs test in September 2003.

This had never happened to a high profile footballer before and for it to involve one of the highest profiled black British player of his generation meant that the incident created even more sensation.

Black football's early pioneers were just happy to get acceptance as human beings. Ferdinand's suspension meant the United defender had to try and regain public trust after missing the test. There was a stage when, mainly due to the media hype, Ferdinand's career was in jeopardy.

No player black or white had been in similar 'trouble' with football's authorities and on occasion observers of the story were not sure if the colour of Ferdinand's skin was a help or a hindrance.

He had been ordered to take a routine FA drugs test at Manchester United's Carrington training ground but he left without undergoing the procedure.

Claiming he forgot because he was moving house at the time and was distracted, he went shopping in Manchester city centre, a pastime for which he has a penchant. Upon discovering his blunder, he later contacted the club to offer to take the test, but was told it was too late as the Football Association's testers had gone. Ferdinand provided a negative urine sample within two days but the issue was not whether he was taking drugs but that he had missed the test.

The whole saga caused a huge debate over how footballers found guilty of drug offences, which includes missing tests, should be treated.

The Strike Partnership

An independent tribunal found him guilty of misconduct and banned him for eight months. It meant that Ferdinand, now a regular in the England side, would miss most of the domestic season and crucially Euro 2004. United appealed against the punishment but to no avail.

Ferdinand returned to action in September 2004 in a match against Liverpool at Old Trafford. Without him United's Premiership chances had floundered. On his return against Liverpool it was easy to see what United had missed.

His pace and ability to read the game came back in an instant. It was if he had never been away. The football adage 'Form is temporary and class is permanent' proved to be correct in Ferdinand's case.

The self-confessed shopaholic, who also enjoys listening to music and reading a good book, has not forgotten his roots. He still does much for the area and community in south east London where he spent his formative years.

He has openly supported issues relevant to the black community including the Damilola Taylor Trust and the Stand Up Speak Up anti-racist football campaign headed by Thierry Henry. When one considers the positive things that Ferdinand involves himself in, his missing the drugs test and the subsequent furore bear no relation.

It has always been easy to applaud the numerous gifted goal scorers that have come from the African-Caribbean community. However, the elegant form of Rio Ferdinand has ensured that now defenders are now also viewed with a healthy respect. Another landmark for black footballers.

Chapter 17

In the Lower Leagues

ONE NAME GUARANTEED to be included in any history of black footballers in England is that of Tony Ford. It has to be there if for no other reason than his longevity in a demanding and physical game.

While Ford has never attracted big headlines and pay packets, his stickability – he has played for the best part of thirty seasons – has put to bed the stupid rumour of old that black players were not in the sport for the long haul.

In January 2000, Ford was awarded the MBE for his services to football and he has since gone on to be the oldest outfield player in the English game, the first to rack up one thousand appearances. To be strictly accurate he made one thousand and one League and Cup appearances and scored one hundred and twenty goals.

In 1998, his devotion to the game was recognised by his peers when he was the recipient of a Professional Footballers' Association 'Special Award.'

For Grimsby-born Ford the problems that some other black players have encountered has never been a real issue.

"I just ignored them [the racists] to be honest. I felt it was the best way forward. I just let it go and it went. It has never been something that has followed me around. I have definitely been lucky in that way.

"I have never really experienced any incidents with racism directed at myself. I can only recount two incidents in my whole life. One was on a football pitch and one was when I actually went to buy a house which is nothing to do with the sport.

"When I was growing up there wasn't a particularly big black community or any other kind of community in Grimsby but I was always accepted and it has certainly helped.

"I didn't really associate myself with being black and wanting to be a black player in football. I just wanted to be a footballer. My colour didn't inspire me to go any further because in my environment, the place where I lived, they accepted me. So I was just another person. I was never seen as the 'black kid'.

"There is no doubt that racism it is still around but sometimes I think it is highlighted just a little bit too much. The game now is probably as cosmopolitan as you can get. I mean you have got every nationality playing football. You have got every colour playing football. It is possibly the best mix you could ever get but it is still disappointing to hear some stories of people who have suffered really bad abuse.

"It is sad when the game still gets dragged down by some of the incidents highlighted in the media."

It was in 1978 that Ford signed professional forms for Grimsby for the first time. He had twelve years with his home town club before starting his football odyssey. He had spells with Sunderland, Stoke City, West Bromwich Albion, Scunthorpe United, Bradford City, Barrow, Mansfield Town and Rochdale Town.

The right-sided midfield player, who recalls that his first weekly pay packet was just £10, reckons he has missed less than one hundred matches during a career which has spanned almost a quarter of a century.

What has been the key to this particular Ford proving to have a very good engine?

"A lot of people ask me this. I enjoyed playing football as a kid and I enjoyed it every time I trained and every time I played. I was fairly competitive as well. I did like the competitive side. It just kept me going. I wasn't trying to break any records or set any record of any kind, I just enjoyed playing."

Grimsby will always have a special place in his heart. Just listening to Ford gives the impression that while he may not be a household name he has achieved everything he set out to do while playing for the club.

"It meant a great deal to me obviously with being a local boy in Grimsby. They were the first professional football team I saw play. I think I was about nine years old when I watched my first game and I just wanted to play for them. I was absolutely delighted and proud to actually become a Grimsby player."

With regard to today's overpaid and pampered footballers, who enjoy celebrity in the same manner as some of Hollywood's top names, Ford says: "I can't be envious because I earned decent money in my time. I think salaries are fantastically inflated but if somebody is prepared to pay them then you can't blame the players for taking them.

"I keep a reasonable grasp on things that are happening. You read the papers. I am still involved in football. I am assistant manager at Rochdale so you do hear lots of things that are going on in football."

Like most players, Ford envisaged a career in management once he hung up his well worn-boots. The player, who cites the legendary Tottenham and England goal-scoring legend Jimmy Greaves among his football idols, is not put off by the lack of opportunity.

"I would perhaps like to get a job as a manager in my own right. Hopefully the opportunity will come along and I will be in the game for as long as I enjoy it, in whatever capacity I possibly can. If I lose the edge from what I do then it will be time to completely call it a day.
"If I could have my time again and know what I know now, I most probably would have made more money. I possibly would have got the agent that I never had. I might have made a move to another club and maybe pushed for some more things, but you don't know.
"The experiences are there as you go along but the best thing for me is that I have enjoyed it for so long. I have been injury free for so long so I can't really say that there are many things that I would change."

And will today's professional footballer be able to replicate Ford's longevity?
"I really don't know because my first appearance was when I was sixteen and my last one was when I was forty-two. Now, if they are going to have people play for twenty-six years to actually get up to that same number of appearances then I think it is possibly very unlikely especially with the strains that are put on the players now.

"The game has got fast and it really does drive the body a lot more. If they can maybe play seventy games a year like Frank Lampard did for Chelsea when they won the Premiership in 2005 maybe yes, but I think it is unlikely."

Chapter 18

Arsenal and the future

IN THE mid-1990s, Arsène Wenger was to project black players into the global spotlight unlike any other coach before him.

Wenger was something of an unknown quantity when he became manager of Arsenal in September 1996. Most observers were left scratching their heads on his appointment asking the question 'Arsène who?' But a decade later he has been acknowledged as a coach who has given the African-Caribbean footballer his chance.

Having gained a reputation at Monaco, where he won the Championship and Manager of the Year awards in the late 1980s, Wenger was also to have an impact on the Japanese game before arriving in the red and white half of north London.

Significantly, even before he had put pen to paper himself, Wenger acquired the services of one Patrick Vieira as the Frenchman's Highbury revolution took early shape. Vieira was to prove to be the first of many black footballers Wenger entrusted to look after the Highbury tradition. Since his signing and subsequent departure, many black players have walked through the club's famous marble halls.

Nicolas Anelka, Luis Boa Morte, Christopher Wreh, Lauren, Kolo Toure, Sol Campbell, Ashley Cole, Gael Clichy, Edu, Sylvain Wiltord, Kanu, Silvinho, Gilberto and Thierry Henry have all played their part as Arsenal's style has grown more expansive since the departure of previous manager George Graham.

Graham, nicknamed Sergeant-Major, certainly brought trophies to Arsenal, aided by black players like Paul Davis, Michael Thomas, David Rocastle, Chris Whyte, Raphael Meade, Gus Caesar and the irrepressible Ian Wright, but his teams did not play with the verve and va-va-voom of Wenger's musketeers.

Wenger is now the most successful Arsenal manager in history, having won seven major honours for the Gunners. In each of the eight full seasons before Chelsea's Russian revolution kicked in, Arsenal had finished in the top two in the Premiership, while also reaching the last four of the FA Cup seven times to confirm their consistency.

While Wenger has proved his penchant for unearthing talent from around the world, it is his discovery of black talent that has truly caught the imagination.

Vieira and Henry have been the icing on Arsenal's highly palatable cake for the best part of a decade. Vieira proved to be the complete midfielder with his athleticism, eye for a pass and the odd goal.

Henry, who could hardly hit a barn door when joining Arsenal from Juventus for £10.5million in 1999, is now just behind the likes of Ronaldinho for the title of best player in the world. And in October 2005, Henry surpassed Wright's goal-scoring record to confirm his own status as legend. But despite Henry's star status it is as a collective that Arsenal have caught the eye and changed the English game beyond recognition.

There was a time when black players were seen to be making up the numbers; not any more. Wenger's vision and trust in black footballers have seemingly made it chic, and essential, to have players of natural physicality and pace in a football team.

Most clubs in the English top flight have a black 'general' in midfield and a lightning quick forward up top. The attributes that the abused pioneers possessed have now been universally accepted as the way to go and Wenger's ability to spot, and play, black players is not to be underestimated.

When Arsenal regained their Premiership crown in 2003-04 they did so in outstanding fashion. They were undefeated throughout the season, the first club to achieve the feat since Preston in the 1800s when the competition was much less intense. Just three games into the 2004-05 season, Wenger's side beat Blackburn Rovers 3-0 to eclipse Nottingham Forest's unbeaten record, making it forty-three matches unbeaten. They would eventually go on to forty-nine matches without a loss.

Even more remarkable in this wonderful story is that Arsenal and Wenger have not had the financial resources to raid the transfer market in the manner of Chelsea and Manchester United. Wenger has made his purchases shrewdly.

There was mixed reaction when Wenger fielded a team with not a single British player in it in February 2005. Football has always been the passionate pastime of the working class. However, people do seem to accept change in football with greater ease than they do in the rest of life. And the success, with the panache that Wenger has brought to Highbury has warded off most of the critics.

An opinion poll of most football fans would show that a successful side full of Brits is still the ideal but success with a foreign line up is now not too far behind.

The progress of non-British and black players has been such over the years that they are now judged by one single criterion, their ability. It is no longer a case of what language they speak or the colour of their skin. And Wenger's Arsenal can take some responsibility for that acceptance.

Wenger might have been responsible for an African/French revolution at Highbury but in 2004 a Russian brought similar change to west London.

Chelsea's billionaire owner Roman Abramovich changed the shape of the Premiership when he arrived at Chelsea. Players were purchased for sums of money not previously witnessed in the English top flight.

At times players were brought two at a time and revealed at the same press conference, each holding aloft a new shirt.

Chelsea are the new force in England, if not Europe. While they have a core of goalkeeper Petr Cech and Englishmen John Terry and Frank Lampard, they have, like Wenger, been reliant on the black footballer.

The knowledgeable football fraternity recognise that Lampard would not be the same player without the stability of Claude Makelele, born in Kinshasha the Democratic Republic of Congo, formerly Zaire.

Makelele moved to Savigny-le-Temple, a Parisian suburb in 1977, when he was just four years old His father was also a football player selected for the Congo DR national football team before ending his career in the Belgian first division.

Makélélé had never left Savigny-le-Temple until the age of sixteen, when he joined the training centre of Brest-Armorique in Brittany. He did not find it easy to adapt to the tough new life in Brest.

Although he worked hard in Brest, it was in Nantes where he discovered the real pleasure of playing.

The football community knew his value, especially when he was at Madrid, as the midfield spoiler who allowed the 'galacticos' to shine. But a lot of his graft went unnoticed even by his employers. So in 2003, after just three seasons, he decided to leave the Santiago Bernabéu because, while Real would not pay him what he thought he was worth, Chelsea would.

At the time of writing (July 2006) Real have won nothing since his departure whereas Chelsea have twice won the Premiership with the promise of more honours.

The first player to be signed under Mourinho's reign was West Ham United's Glen Johnson for £6million in July 2003 and other black players followed. Add Didier Drogba (£24million) and Michael Essien (£31million) and the opinions of some Chelsea fans about black footballers have had to change.

The attitudes at Stamford Bridge are now a long way from the days of Paul Canoville, the first black player to don a Chelsea first team shirt.

Canoville was subjected to awful abuse during his playing days in the 1980s. Chelsea attracted a large number of hardcore racists in those days and Canoville had to display immense strength of character and dignity to win over a large section of his own so-called supporters who vilified him regularly in the months following his debut. Things got so bad, and obviously had such an effect on Canoville's confidence, that it took some very public support from the then chairman Ken Bates to give the player the boost he needed at that time. Those very same Chelsea fans who were obviously disgusted that a black man was representing their beloved club now cheer the present team. How times have changed.

The fact that Chelsea would not be where they are

today – as possibly the world's most powerful club thanks to Russian roubles – without black players must bring a smile to not only Canoville's face but those of every black player that has ever been abused by their own fans.

It would be too easy for young football fans to think that black players have always been welcome at Chelsea and other clubs at home and abroad. But they have not.

The changing of the guard at Stamford Bridge and Highbury is key to the continued bid to kick racism out of football.

This book has chronicled the fortunes of some of the black players that have made their mark in British/ English football's rich heritage.

Among their number have been a fair few players who have played for England. However, as we know, some have found wearing the Three Lions on their chest to be a chastening experience. Luther Blissett, John Barnes, Cyrille Regis, Andrew Cole and Ian Wright all suffered.

But football, like life, is made up of many ironies. Clyde Best fought single-handedly for recognition from 1969-1976 at West Ham. But a look at West Ham's Championship play-off final line up in May 2005 shows that seven black players represented a club which was one of the worst offenders when it came to racism. West Ham's line-up included Anton Ferdinand, Chris Powell, Shaun Newton, Nigel Reo-Coker, Hayden Mullins, Marlon Harewood and Bobby Zamora. Add the fact that Reo-Coker, with Sierre Leone roots, captained United in the absence of the veteran Teddy Sheringham and that Bobby Zamora scored the crucial second half goal to give his club victory in the Championship play-off final in the Millennium

Stadium and Best's battle thirty years before can be seen to have been won. And that battle was not just for players at West Ham but for those in the rest of the United Kingdom and beyond.

The national team, the crown jewels in England's football crown, would appear to be making the same positive steps. The black footballer who represented England in the 1970s, '80s and '90s was an easy target because he was generally in isolation. That is no longer the case.

Black players are now taking to the field on merit and a cursory glance at the various academies in England suggests that the conveyor belt of talent is unlikely to break down.

One of the players who could be a real star in South Africa in the World Cup of 2010 is Jermain Defoe. The Tottenham forward made an impressive start to his international career and he is ultra-keen to prove himself on the world stage by staying determined and focused. He made the most impressive of international starts by scoring against Poland in a crucial World Cup qualifier in September 2004.

Defoe said:

> "When you are a forward, when you are scoring goals, it is all you want to do really. That is the thing you think about. As for the England game, when I found out that I was starting I thought 'right I just want to play and play well.' Play well and work hard for the team. It was a big game, so I was glad to be a part of that. To score the goal was just a dream come true."

Defoe shot to prominence as a youth player with Charlton Athletic. Controversially he was to sign for West Ham United in July 1999 for £1.5million, having never played for Charlton. United loaned their rising star to Bournemouth from October 2000 to May 2001 and it was while on the South Coast that Defoe was to really show his pedigree.

He was to score in eleven consecutive Football League matches for Bournemouth, a Football League record. In February 2004 he left West Ham in the transfer window to join Tottenham Hotspur for £7million and he has since cemented his reputation at domestic level. Now he seeks now to do the same on a bigger stage.

While the irrepressible Wayne Rooney and Michael Owen are England's first-choice strikers, Defoe, however, understood that he had to be patient in order to get his chance.

"Since I have been playing I have always worked hard and stay on after training to do extra, just trying to get there really. When you are growing up and you are young and you watch the Premiership and you watch all the great players a lot of them set you an example. You watch all the English games and when you are young you just want to be a part of that. To be a part of it now is great. You try not to get complacent and just keep your feet on the ground and just keep working hard and pushing on."

Add the likes of Aaron Lennon, Jermaine Jenas, Darren Bent, Kieran Richardson, Anton Ferdinand, and, of course, Theo Walcott and the revolution if not exactly complete continues to gather significant momentum.

Walcott became the most expensive sixteen-year-old in the history of British football when he moved to Arsenal for a fee which could rise to £12million and caused a sensation when he was inexplicably chosen

Arsenal and the future

in England manager Sven Goran Eriksson's final World Cup squad that took part in the tournament in Germany. Walcott was chosen by Eriksson even though he had not made a Premiership start for his club.

Having blown away the stereotypes of yesteryear and proved that they can actually play in the cold, defend, lead a team and play in a unit and withstand the brutish physicality of the game, it has been mooted that for England to claim back football's Holy Grail and replicate their 1966 World Cup win it will take eleven black men.

The England under-21 side which almost qualified for the 2006 European Championships was once again top-heavy with black players. Reo-Coker, a real star in the making and a genuine contender to lead the senior team, was missing from the two-legged semi-final against France but the rest of the team sheet would have brought a smile to Watson, Wharton, Tull and the rest.

Anton Ferdinand, Nedum Onuoha, Tom Huddlestone, Kieran Richardson, Darren Bent and Carlton Cole made up the hub of the under-21 side and luck with injuries and continued commitment could see them eventually replace the team that strived for glory at the World Cup in Germany in the summer of 2006.

And among the England schoolboys that ended sharing the Victory Shield with Wales in November 2005 was a host of black teenage talent. Teenagers who impressed for England in the Victory Shield included Danny Rose and Tom Taiwo (Leeds United), Victor Moses (Crystal Palace) and Jordan Spence (West Ham United). This quartet should prove to be the next crop of hugely gifted footballers.

A look at some of the players presently representing

top Premiership clubs – the exclusive England club normally comes from this small pool – points to, with added maturity and experience, a real chance of success in South Africa if a coach can be found to gel the combined talents.

The only question remaining is will the powers-that-be at Football Association's headquarters in London's Soho Square permit such radical change?

Vivek Chaudhary alleged in the *Guardian* in 2004 that a former England manager was once told during his tenure not to pick too many black players.

Chaudhary said that ironically the comments were made during a 10th anniversary lunch to mark the work of the Kick It Out. The claims were never substantiated but as football's first ever World Cup in Africa draws closer is it too much to expect that such archaic thinking will be put to bed once and for all?

Will black players be judged on their ability rather than be embroiled in the controversy that an England XI made up solely of black players would obviously generate?

Such a radical step has to be in doubt, but those types of negative thought processes, you would think, should belong to the bad old days when the likes of Watson, Wharton, Tull and Best played. But as Piara Powar, the director of Kick It Out, has intimated, while progress has been made there is still some work to be done with football's race relations.

However, unlike the black football pioneers, the new generations look on course to get their dues. Typical English names such as John and Paul have been replaced by modern black names such as Jermaine. It is not only a sign of the times but a reminder that those who had to put up with the most severe humanitarian issues have won their battle and allowed a new, vibrant and talented generation to, in the main, concentrate on football matters.

The stereotypes that sullied black players have been blown away. Leadership, vision and physicality are very much part of their football make-up. To emphasise the point, a third of the Premiership had black players as their captains at the end of 2005.

It is no longer simply a matter of colour.

Other books from SportsBooks

Wembley – The Complete Record 1923–2000

Glen Isherwood

Every football match ever played at the world's most iconic football stadium is detailed in this exhaustive reference work.
Paperback. ISBN 1899807 42 X £14.99

Ha'Way/Howay the Lads

Alan Candlish

A fascinating and detailed history of the rivalry between Newcastle United and Sunderland.
Paperback. ISBN 1899807 39 X £14.99

Ode to Jol

Alasdair Gold

A sideways, and very funny, look at Tottenham Hotspurs' 2005/06 season.
Paperback. ISBN 1899807 43 8 £12.99

Accrington Stanley - the club that wouldn't die

Phil Whalley

Accrington Stanley returned to the Football League this year after resigning in 1962. This tells the story of the years of struggle and eventual triumph.
Hardback. ISBN 1899807 47 0 £16.99

Harry Potts – Margaret's Story

Margaret Potts and Dave Thomas

Harry Potts was Burnley's manager in the days the small-town team won the league and reached the FA Cup final. Great photographic section.
Hardback. ISBN 1899807 41 1 £17.99

Fitba Gaullimaufry

Adam Scott

Everything you need to know, and some things you don't about Scottish football. Hardback. ISBN 1899807 45 4 £9.99

Growing up with Subbuteo – my dad invented the world's greatest football game

Mark Adolph

Tells the story of growing up with his father Peter, the man who invented Subbuteo. A very funny, often poignant account of life with an eccentric father. Paperback. ISBN 1899807 40 3 £7.99

Willie Irvine – Together Again

Willie Irvine with Dave Thomas

The remarkable story of the Burnley and Northern Ireland centre forward who grew up in abject poverty, rose to the heights only to fall into depression after he stopped playing. Hardback. ISBN 1899807 33 0 £17.99

Twickenham – the History of the Cathedral of Rugby

Ed Harris

The story of rugby's most famous ground, from its days as a cabbage patch to a multi-million pound sports arena. Hardback. ISBN 1899807 29 2 £17.99

Europe United – a History of the European Cup/Champions League

Andrew Godsell

The European Cup and its successor, the Champions League, was 50 years old in 2005 and this book celebrates all the great games and characters of the world's greatest club compeition.
Hardback. ISBN 1899807 30 6 Price £17.99

Another Bloody Tangle!

Peter Bishop

The author loves fishing, sadly the sport doesn't reciprocate. Just before publication, Peter won his first competition and then when the cup was presented promptly dropped it. Paperback. ISBN 1899807 28 4 £7.99

The Art of Bradman

Difficult to find a new book about the greatest batsman ever. But this is unique. A selection of paintings of the great man from the Bradman Museum at Bowral Oval with text by the museum's curator. Leatherbound with gold lettering and red ribbon marker. ISBN 1899807 32 2 £25

Colin Blythe – lament for a legend

Christopher Scoble

Colin Blythe was a giant in the golden age of county cricket before the First World War and this is the first biography of a complex personality, who was one of the first cricketers to challenge the game's rulers, demanding to handle his own financial affairs. Hardback. ISBN 1899807 31 4 £16.99

Test Cricket Grounds

John Woods

For dedicated cricket fans who plan to watch their country play overseas. Woods spent a year and a day visiting all 58 grounds that stage Test cricket. Wisden International Cricket magazine called it "a bible for the Barmy Army... perfect..." Paperback. ISBN 1899807 20 9 £12.99

Raich Carter – the biography

Frank Garrick

Raich Carter is the only man to win FA Cup winners' medals before and after the Second World War. Published to commemorate the 10th anniversary of his death. The Times said: "leaves the reader in no doubt about the nature of Carter's genius". Hardback. ISBN 1899807 18 7 £16.99